外贸英语函电

主　编　赵春漫
副主编　章艳华　孙宝凤
参　编　丁　卫　王艳会

内 容 简 介

本书共分 11 章。第 1 章简要介绍外贸信函的基本要素、格式和写作原则。第 2~10 章讲授外贸进出口流程的主要环节：建立业务关系、询盘与回复、报盘与还盘、达成交易、支付、包装、装运、保险、投诉与索赔等，侧重于对该外贸环节中最常用的几类信函的介绍。每章分为若干个针对外贸环节的具体写作任务，包括概述、写作技巧、信函实例、有用的表达和典型句型、实训项目、选择性的学习材料和课后习题。第 11 章简要介绍传真和电子邮件的基本要素和写作要点。

本书适用于高等职业技术学院、继续教育学院等大专层次的国际贸易、商务英语、国际商务等相关专业的教学及外贸行业的培训，也可供从事国际交流和对外贸易的从业人员自学或参考。

图书在版编目（CIP）数据

外贸英语函电/赵春漫主编．—北京：北京大学出版社，2011.2
（全国高职高专国际商务类规划教材）
ISBN 978-7-301-18016-7

Ⅰ.①外… Ⅱ.①赵… Ⅲ.①对外贸易—英语—电报信函—写作—高等学校：技术学校—教材 Ⅳ.①H315

中国版本图书馆 CIP 数据核字（2010）第 213068 号

书　　　名：	外贸英语函电
著作责任者：	赵春漫　主编
策 划 编 辑：	成　淼
责 任 编 辑：	陈　薇
标 准 书 号：	ISBN 978-7-301-18016-7/F・2634
出 版 者：	北京大学出版社
地　　　址：	北京市海淀区成府路 205 号　100871
网　　　址：	http://www.pup.cn　新浪官方微博：@北京大学出版社
电　　　话：	邮购部 62752015　发行部 62750672　编辑部 62754934　出版部 62754962
电 子 信 箱：	zyjy@pup.cn
印 刷 者：	三河市博文印刷有限公司
发 行 者：	北京大学出版社
经 销 者：	新华书店
	787 毫米×1092 毫米　16 开本　14.25 印张　336 千字
	2011 年 2 月第 1 版　2021 年 3 月第 5 次印刷
定　　　价：	28.00 元

未经许可，不得以任何方式复制或抄袭本书之部分或全部内容。
版权所有，侵权必究
举报电话：010-62752024；电子信箱：fd@pup.pku.edu.cn

前　言

　　本书着眼于新世纪条件下的高等职业教育，遵循高等职业教育培养应用技术型人才的要求，注重培养学生对基础知识的应用能力。本书符合基于工作过程的职业教育特点，以岗位职业能力为切入点，结合教学与工作过程，设计教、学、做三者合一的教学情境，以任务为驱动，使学生在模拟实际操作中培养和提高解决实际问题的能力与专业技能。每一章的工作任务都是外贸业务员岗位的核心工作程序，全部来自真实的工作环境。通过真实的工作任务训练，能够使学生最终熟练掌握工作流程的操作，熟悉相关的知识，并在潜移默化中形成本岗位所需要的知识、素质和职业能力。

　　本书共分 11 章。第 1 章简要介绍外贸信函的基本要素、格式和写作原则。第 2～10 章讲授外贸进出口流程的主要环节：建立业务关系、询盘与回复、报盘与还盘、达成交易、支付、包装、装运、保险、投诉与索赔等，侧重于对该外贸环节中最常用的几类信函的介绍。每章分为若干个针对该外贸环节的具体写作任务，具体包括：概述、写作技巧、信函实例、有用的表达和典型句型、实训项目、选择性的学习材料和课后习题。其中，概述部分介绍写信的目的及相关的业务背景知识；写作技巧部分介绍此类信函的写作结构和注意事项；信函实例部分提供 4～6 个典型范例，每例各有侧重，每封样信后都附有相关注释；有用的表达和典型句型部分提供一些较常用的语句供学生写作参考；实训项目部分提供 2～3 个针对该业务环节的项目训练，供学生练笔之用；选择性的学习材料部分包含对该章的相关补充信息和信函实例；课后习题部分以专业词汇、习惯表达、情景写作等练习内容为主，提供形式多样的练习，巩固课堂所学知识。第 11 章简要介绍传真和电子邮件的基本要素和写作要点。

　　本书的创新点有以下几个：

　　1. 基于工作过程：本书的内容主要是根据进出口贸易的整个流程选取的，是外贸业务流程中最核心的内容，是完成业务磋商与达成的必要步骤。因此，本课程教学内容完全是针对实际的工作过程，学生学习完本课程可以自如地应对外贸公司的基本业务，并可以熟练完成英语信函的翻译与撰写，独立承担业务。

　　2. 任务驱动型：邀请行业专家明确外贸岗位所包含的工作过程和任务，在任务分析的基础上，确定以任务为导向的课程方案，教学内容按任务模块进行组织，教学程序采用任务驱动方式，以项目、任务引领，采取教、学、做一体的教学模式，加强对学生外贸操作技能的训练。

3. 突出实用性：紧密结合我国外贸业务的实际情况，突出实用性和针对性，系统训练学生撰写书信和处理信息的能力。

4. 加强操作性：本教材编写的原则是精讲多练，每一章都附有实训项目，强调对学生的商务写作实践能力的培养。以加强素质教育、提高学生综合能力为目标，巩固学生英语语言知识及外贸业务知识，注重理论与实践相结合，教学内容突出系统性，并在加强与其他课程协调方面进行探索与尝试。

另外本书附有相关课件和练习答案，可在出版社网站（http://www.pup.cn/dl/）下载。

本书主要编写人员有赵春漫、章艳华、孙宝凤、丁卫、王艳会等，江苏安邦集团外经公司姚娟为本书提供了实训材料，对此表示感谢。

由于编者水平有限，书中难免存在不足之处，敬请读者批评指正。

编　者
2011 年 1 月

目 录

Chapter 1　Basic Knowledge and Layout of a Business Letter 1

Chapter 2　Establishing Business Relations 18

　　Task 1　Establishment of Business Relations 19
　　Task 2　Credit & Status Enquiries 24

Chapter 3　Enquiry and Reply 38

　　Task 1　Making an Enquiry 39
　　Task 2　Reply to an Enquiry 42

Chapter 4　Offer and Counter-offer 55

　　Task 1　Making an Offer 56
　　Task 2　Making a Counter-offer 58

Chapter 5　Conclusion of Business 72

　　Task 1　Placing an Order 73
　　Task 2　Accepting an Order 76
　　Task 3　Declining an Order 78

Chapter 6　Terms of Payment 90

　　Task 1　Negotiating Payment Terms 91
　　Task 2　Urging & Advising Establishment of an L/C 97
　　Task 3　Requesting to Amend an L/C 105

Chapter 7　Packing 127

　　Task 1　Informing Packing Requirements 128
　　Task 2　Reply to Packing Issues 131

Chapter 8　Shipment 146

　　Task 1　Giving Shipping Instructions 147
　　Task 2　Urging a Timely Shipment 149
　　Task 3　Giving Shipping Advice 151
　　Task 4　Asking for an Amendment to Shipment Clause 153

外贸英语函电

Chapter 9　Insurance 165
Task 1　Requesting the Exporter to Cover Insurance 166
Task 2　Type of Coverage Adopted 169
Task 3　Reply to the Letter Requesting Excessive Insurance 171

Chapter 10　Complaint and Claim 182
Task 1　Making Complaints or Claims 183
Task 2　Reply to Complaints and Claims 188

Chapter 11　Fax & E-mail 203

附录　外贸函电常用词汇 216

参考文献 222

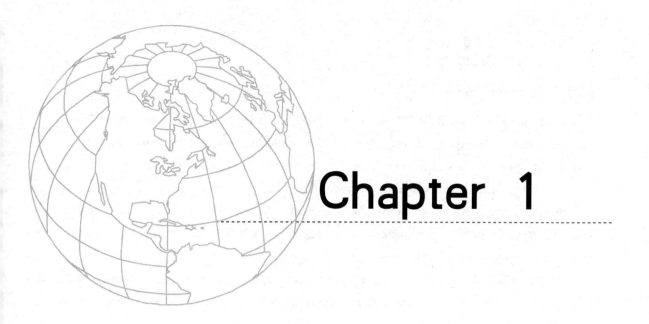

Chapter 1

Basic Knowledge and Layout of a Business Letter

Part I. Introduction

Communication is the lifeline of modern business. Among the different forms of communication, business letter is the most frequently used. So, we should be quite familiar with the established format and features of business letters in order to communicate effectively.

A business letter is also called business correspondence, which is used to convey meanings and directions among businessmen in their trades. Broadly speaking, the functions of a business letter are to ask for or to convey business information, to make or to accept an offer, to deal with matters concerning various businesses.

A successful letter is one that wins a favorable response— the success of the letter is judged by the response. Let the response you desire be your guide throughout the letter. You should take the following tips:

1. Stating your purpose of writing clearly

2. Writing with exact words

3. Keeping business letter formal and factual

4. You-attitude: let your reader's interest be your guide in selecting and phrasing of ideas.

5. Expression skills: try to use expressions in English that are clear, persuasive, natural, thoughtful, and interesting.

Usually, there are certain essential requirements for a good business letter, which can be summed up in the Seven Cs: Completeness, Concreteness, Clearness/Clarity, Conciseness, Courtesy, Consideration, Correctness. These Cs often go hand-in-hand.

1. Completeness

A business communication should include all the necessary information. It is essential to check the message carefully before it is sent out to see that all the matters are discussed, and all the questions are answered. Business letters should avoid incompleteness.

2. Concreteness

Concreteness means making the message specific, definite and vivid. Business letters should avoid being too general. In general letters, everything seems to be mentioned but actually few are fully expounded. You should use specific facts and figures, vivid and image-building words.

3. Clearness/Clarity

Make sure that your letter is so clear that it cannot be misunderstood. A point that is ambiguous in a letter will cause trouble to both sides, and further exchange of letters for explanation will become inevitable, thus time will be lost. You must try to express yourself clearly. To achieve this, you should keep in mind the purpose of your letter and use appropriate

Chapter 1 Basic Knowledge and Layout of a Business Letter

words in correct sentence structures to fully convey your meaning. When you are sure about what you want to say, say it in plain, simple words. Short, familiar, conversational and straightforward English is what is needed for business letters.

4. Conciseness

Conciseness is often considered to be the most important writing principle. A concise letter is not necessarily a short one. Conciseness means stating things in the fewest possible words. To achieve this, try to avoid wordiness or redundancy. Clearness and conciseness often go hand-in-hand and the elimination of wordy business jargon can help to make a letter clearer and at the same time more concise. Generally speaking, you will gain clearness and conciseness by writing short sentences rather than long ones.

5. Courtesy

Courtesy is not mere politeness. The courteous writer should be sincere and tactful, and thoughtful. You need to prepare every message with the readers in mind and try to put yourself into their places. Promptness is one of the most important things in being courteous. Punctuality will please your customer who dislikes waiting a long time for a reply.

6. Consideration

Consideration means you should be considerate to your readers. It is the quality that enables us to refuse a customer's request without killing all hopes of future business. Generally, the native English writers lay great emphasis on the "you" attitude. "You-attitude" is not so simple as only to use "you" instead of "I" or "we". In your letters you should always keep in mind the persons you are writing to, try to see things from their points of view, see their problems and difficulties and express your ideas in terms of their experience. "You-attitude" can help to avoid an awkward situation, and promote cooperation between the trading parties. If you cannot meet your customers' needs or requests, you should show your interest in and concern for their requests, using positive sentences instead of using negative sentences, and stress what you can do instead of what you cannot do.

7. Correctness

Business letters must be correct, otherwise they may be misunderstood and run the risk of reaching nowhere or going astray. Correctness means appropriate and grammatically correct language (without spelling or typographical errors) and factual information that is accurate with reliable figures such as names of articles, specifications, quantity, and unit price.

This book mainly dwells on 9 types of business correspondence that are widely used in foreign trade, which are about: establishing business relations, enquiry & reply, offer & counter offer, conclusion of business, terms of payment, packing, shipment, insurance, and complaint & claim.

Part II. Parts of a Business Letter

Necessary Parts of a Business Letter:

1. heading or letter head	信头
2. date	日期
3. inside name and address	信内名称和地址
4. salutation	称呼
5. letter body	正文
6. complimentary close	结尾敬语
7. signature	签名

Optional Parts of a Business Letter:

8. reference number	编号/参考号
9. attention line	经办人
10. subject line /caption	事由
11. reference notation	经办人代号
12. cnclosure	附件
13. carbon copy notation (distribution notation)	抄送
14. postscript/P.S.	附言

1. Reference Number

The reference number is generally used as a useful indication for filing and consulting for both sides, so it must be easily seen. It may include a file number, a contract number, an L/C number or initials of the signer and the typist's initials. People usually mark "Our ref:" and "Your ref:" to avoid confusion. The position of the reference number is often one or two lines below letterhead.

2. Attention Line

The phrase "For the attention of…" or simply "Attention" is used where the writer of a letter addressing to an organization. The writer wishes to send the letter to a particular person. It should be two lines below the inside address. It is usually placed at the left margin, but occasionally centered on the page.

3. Subject Line

The subject line is often inserted between the salutation and the body of the letter, either beginning at the left margin or the centre, depending on which style you are using. The subject line helps to invite attention to the topic of the letter. It is especially useful if two companies have a lot of correspondence with each other on a variety of subjects, as it immediately tells what the letter is about. It is also useful as a guide for filing. It can begin with or without "Re:" or "Subject:". Sometimes, you can see the subject line is underlined. No matter what the form is, it should always denote what the letter is about.

    e.g. Re: Sewing Machines

        Subject: Sewing Machines

        Sewing Machines

4. Reference Notation

The reference notations are made up of the initials of the person who dictates the letter and of the secretary or typist. The initials are usually typed two lines below the signature at the left margin. The two sets are separated by a colon or a slant, with the dictator's coming first. You may capitalize both, or neither, or only the first of the set.

    e.g. LJ/JS   LJ:JS   LJ:js   LJ/js

5. Enclosure

If any documents such as catalogues, price lists, order, copies of fax, etc. are sent with a letter, it is necessary to add enclosure notation to remind the receiver. The enclosure notation is usually placed two lines below the signature at the left margin. The marking may be in any of the following ways:

    e.g. Enclosure: 3 copies of...   Encl.: 3 catalogues

        Enc.: 1 invoice   Encls: a/s (as stated)

6. Carbon Copy Notation

If the copy of the letter is to be sent to a third party or other people, type cc or CC two lines below the enclosure at the left margin, followed by the name of the recipient of the copy. Its communication function is to indicate to the target reader(s) that someone else is to receive a copy of the same letter. The marking may be in any of the following ways, c.c./cc/bcc (blind carbon copy), e.g., c.c.: Mr. J. Cooper.

7. Postscript/P.S.

A postscript is an afterthought which we should try to avoid using, as in formal letters this is usually a sign of poor planning. If something is forgotten, it is better for the writer to rewrite the whole letter. But as a special device, it has two legitimate functions:

(1) Some executives, to add a personal touch to their typewritten letter, occasionally add a postscript in pen and ink.

(2) Writers of sales letters often withhold one last convincing argument for emphatic inclusion in a postscript.

Sample of a Business Letter:

HANGZHOU GREAT FIBRE PRODUCTS
IMP. & EXP. CORPORATION
Tel: (0571)85497602   E-mail: hzgreatfibre@yahoo.com.cn

信头：*The letter head is usually printed on the top centre or typed on the left of the paper.*

Your Ref: 64/LMG
Our Ref: HZGF/WXG
May 15, 2009

编号和日期：*The reference may include a file number, departmental code or the initials of the signer followed by that of the typist of the letter. All number form (e.g.10/9/2009) should not be used.*

SMITH &SV IMP.& EXP. CORPORATION
NO.968 Fairyland Street
New York, NY 1122
U.S.A.
Attention: Import Dept.

信内名称和地址：*It appears on the left margin and is usually put at least two lines below the date.*

经办人（指明收信人）：*The attention line is used to name the specific individual the letter is addressed to.*

Dear Sirs,   称呼

Subject: Reply to Enquiring   事由

We are writing to tell you that we don't have enough in stock for FCE-5037 you enquired on May 13. It will take us at least 15 days to produce the amount of goods you want, so we are afraid that we can't match your schedule. We have decided not to take your orders.   正文

Thank you for your inquiry, and we will send you information of our new products in case you have any needs.

We hope we can get a chance to cooperate in the near future.

Yours faithfully,   结尾敬语

Chapter 1 Basic Knowledge and Layout of a Business Letter

M.H.Li
Manager

签名

MHL/E.D.

经办人代码

Encl.: as stated

附件

CC: Our Branch Offices

抄送

P.S.: Your letter of April 2 has just arrived. We will look into the matter and reply to you soon.

附言

Part III. Layout of a Business Letter

There are three main formats of a business letter in use at present: the conventional indented style, the modern full block style and the semi-blocked style. The indented style is a traditional British practice. It looks attractive and makes for easy reading, but it is not convenient to type. The full block style is an American style, and it is popular because it is compact and tidy. It is convenient for people to type. The semi-blocked style is a kind of way to write letters in part of full block style and part of indented style. It is an eclectic style that is widely used in international trade.

1. Indented Style（缩行式）

1) Each line of the inside name and address is indented 2 or 3 spaces.

2) Date is placed in the right upper corner of a letter; signature appears in the bottom right-hand corner.

3) The first line of each paragraph should be indented 3-8 spaces to the right from the left margin.

Sample of Indented Style

Beijing Textiles Import & Export Corporation
No.66 Tung An Men Street
Tel: 010-6683812 Telex: 3358711 Cable: 8898

January 30, 2010

Our ref. No.:AX09

    Your ref. No.:PJA32

        The Pakistan Trading Company,

           No.15 Broad Street, Karachi, Pakistan.

Dear Sir,

    We learn from a friend in San Francisco that you are exporting Nylon Bed-sheets and

Pillow Cases. There is a steady demand here for the above-mentioned commodities of high quality at moderate prices.

Should you please send us a copy of your catalogue with your latest prices and terms of payment? We should find it most helpful if you could also supply samples of these goods.

Yours very truly,
BEIJING TEXTILES
IMPORT &. EXPORT CORP.
Zhang Dahua
Import Dept.

2. Full Block Style (齐头式或平头式)

(1) Every line in the full-block style begins at the left margin, including the date, the inside address, each paragraph of the body and the complimentary close.

(2) When using the full block style to write a letter, you should first provide your own address, then skip a line and provide the date, then skip one more line and provide the inside address of the addressee.

Sample of Full Blocked Style

GUANGZHOU ELECTRONICS PRODUCTS
IMPORT&. ECPORT CORPORATION
N0.11 Beijing Road, Guangzhou
People's Republic of China
Tel: 08602083456182   Fax: 08602083456543

Our Ref.: GEC 9667

June 21, 2010

Exclin Electronics Products Import Corp.

130 Margaret Street

London, W1W 8SR

United Kingdom

Dear Sirs,

Re: Chinese Electronics Products

We have obtained your name and address from the London Chamber of Commerce, who have told us that you wish to import electric goods manufactured in China.

Chapter 1 Basic Knowledge and Layout of a Business Letter

We manufacture electric appliances of which illustrated in the enclosed catalogue. We hope it will be of your interest. We also send our latest price list for your reference is.

If you are interested in any of our product, please let us know and we will provide you with a quotation. In the meantime, should you require any further information about either our products or our corporation, please do not hesitate to let us know.

We hope there is a possibility of doing business with you in the future.

Yours faithfully,
Wang Xin
Sales Manager

3. Semi-Blocked Style (混合式)

This style of writing a business letter was applied in universe. Inside address and salutation followed the ways of full block style (type from the left margin). Body is written in indented style. Date, complimentary closure and signature are typed from the center of a line of a letter.

Sample of Semi-Blocked Style 1

Huai'an Futai Import & Export Corporation
No.1356 Pujiang Road
Tel:008651796881268   Fax: 008651716589711

Our Ref. No.:FT1011
Your Ref. No.:AH-DV-102

January 23, 2010

The Pakistan Trading Company,
66, St. Karmi Street, Karachi, Pakistan.
Dear Sir,

  We have been told by Mr. John Smith, the importing manager of DE Company, that your corporation specializes in the export of various light industrial products, and that you are keen to extend your overseas trade. We are, therefore, contacting you with a view to introducing some of your products into our market.

  We have been in the import and export business for over twenty years and have extensive distribution throughout South China. It appears that demand for light industrial products is now increasing and we believe that there is a possibility that your corporation could do considerable business in this area.

At the moment, we are particularly interested in bicycle, and we could appreciate it very much if you could send us your latest catalogues of bicycles as well as price lists.

Yours sincerely,
Zhang Wenshan
Manager

Sample of Semi-Blocked Style 2

GUANGZHOU ELECTRONICS PRODUCTS
IMPORT&. ECPORT CORPORATION
N0.11 Beijing Road, Guangzhou
People's Republic of China
Tel: 00862083456182　　Fax: 00862083456543

Your Ref: TBL/xm
Our Ref: GEC 9556
June 26, 2010
49-51Portland Place
London. W1N 3AH. UK
Dear Mr. Lewis,

　　Your letter of May 22 enquiring about the possibility of importing China-made electronics goods into The UK has been passed on to us by The Ministry of Foreign Economic Relations and Trade in Beijing.

　　We are a state enterprise, and keen to expand our foreign trade. As yet, we have no business contacts in The UK, and would be pleased to consider any business proposals you may have. We enclosed our latest illustrated catalogue together with our latest price lists and terms and conditions of sales for your information. We shall be pleased to deal with any specific enquiries you may have concerning any of our products.

　　Should you require any further details about any of the above-mentioned points, please do not hesitate to contact us.

　　We look forward to hearing from you in the near future.

Yours sincerely,
Wang Qing he
Export Manag

Encls.: As stated

Chapter 1 Basic Knowledge and Layout of a Business Letter

Part IV. Layout of an Envelope

Addressing an envelope correctly helps to ensure that your letter gets to its destination on time. The sender's name and address should be placed in the upper left corner, while the receiver's name and address should be placed about half way down the envelope.

Generally speaking, the name and address of the envelope should in accordance with the inside name and address. It should be written in the following order:

- Name
- Title (position or department)
- Company name
- Street address
- Town
- County (or province)
- Country

Sample of Block Style

Please take a look at the following envelope. George Johnson is writing to the IBM Corporation asking for the latest price list of its products. You can notice that the letter from George Johnson is addressed to IBM Corporation, so there is no specific name of the addressee.

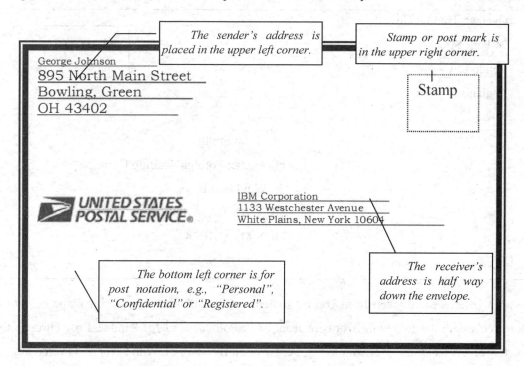

Sample of Indented Style

When a letter is mailed to a third person (or an organization) who is bound to pass it onto the addressee, it is necessary to write the third person's (or the organization's) name down below the addressee's with words "care of" (c/o) in front of it. For example, if an Englishman named John Smith has come to the Hunan Foreign Trading Corp. in China, his own company in England should write to him "care of" (c/o) the Hunan Foreign Trading Corp. which he is staying with.

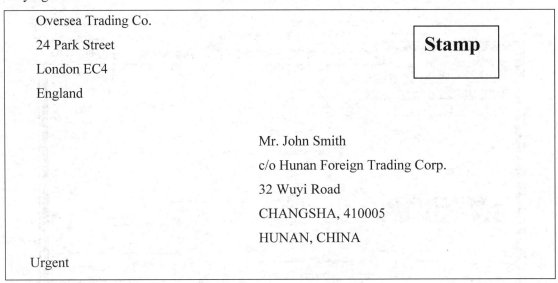

If a letter is to be taken from you by someone to the addressee, write his name below the addressee's with the following words in front of it: Politeness of (or Kindness of, Through the Courtesy of, Per Kindness of, Forwarded by, Per Favor of, By Favor of, With Favor of, Favored by).

Chapter 1 Basic Knowledge and Layout of a Business Letter

```
Oversea Trading Co.
24 Park Street                                    Stamp
London EC4
England


                        Mr. John Smith
                        Kindness of Mr. Zhang Ming

Private
```

Part V. **Useful Expressions and Typical Sentences**

1. We hope to receive a favorable reply.

2. We await the favor of your early (prompt) reply.

3. A prompt reply would greatly oblige us.

4. We trust you will favor us with an early (prompt) reply.

5. We should be obliged by your early (prompt) reply.

6. Will you kindly inform us immediately what you wish us to do?

7. We request you to inform us of your decision by return of post.

8. We are waiting (anxious to receive) your early reply.

9. We thank you for the anticipated favor of your early reply.

10. We thank you in anticipation of your usual courteous prompt attention.

11. We hope to receive your reply with the least possible delay.

12. Kindly reply at your earliest convenience.

13. Please send your reply by the earliest delivery.

14. Please write to us by tonight's mail, without fail.

15. May we remind you that we are still awaiting your early reply?

16. A prompt reply would help us greatly.

17. A prompt reply will greatly oblige us.

18. Your prompt reply would be greatly appreciated.

19. We look forward to receiving your early reply.

20. As the matter is urgent, an early reply will oblige.

21. Good luck!

22. Best wishes!

23. Take care of yourself, will you?

24. Send my love to your…

25. Please write to me when you have time.

26. Please write soon.

27. Let's keep in touch.

28. I am looking forward to your next letter soon.

29. Thank you for an early reply.

30. Please tell me if you need my help.

Part VI. Optional Study

Guidelines of Writing a Business Letter:

- When using the full blocked style, you do not indent paragraphs, including the address of the person you are writing to at the top of the letter, below your company address.
- After the address, double space and include the date.
- State a reference reason for your letter (e.g. "With reference to our telephone conversation...").
- Give the reason for writing (e.g. "I am writing to you to confirm our order...").
- Make any request you may have (e.g. "I would be grateful if you could include a brochure...").
- If there is to be further contact, refer to this contact (e.g. "I look forward to meeting you at...").
- Close the letter with a "thank you" (e.g. "Thank you for your prompt help...").
- Finish the letter with a salutation (e.g. "Yours sincerely").
- Include 4 spaces and type your full name and title.
- Sign the letter between the salutation and the typed name and title.

Part VII. Exercises

I. Translate the following words or phrases into Chinese:

1. letter-head

2. the inside name and address

3. salutation

4. the body of the letter

5. complimentary close

6. signature

Chapter 1 Basic Knowledge and Layout of a Business Letter

7. subject
8. enclosure
9. reference number
10. date
11. indented style
12. block style
13. semi-blocked Style

II. Write business letters according to the clues:

Situation 1: Victor is a company which operates on clothes business. Victor ordered a FCG-32 from Clive Company on May 17, 2006. Unfortunately, that Clive didn't deliver the goods on time caused Victor suffering great losses. Now suppose you are the manager of Victor, write a letter to Clive and ask them to take responsibility for your losses.

Situation 2: Suppose you are the manager of Clive, now you have received a letter from Victor. They ask your repaying to their losses which caused by your faults.

III. Write the inside address:

美国马萨诸塞州(Massachusetts or Mass.)剑桥市(Cambridge)麻省理工学院计算机工程系 John. Smith 教授，邮编：02139

IV. Put the following letters into Full Block Style:

Shangwei Imp/Exp Corporation
112 North Chang'an Rd.
Xi'an, China
Fax: 86-29-85221313
http://www.goodwill.biz.com.cn

Our ref.No.: SHXGW2007-0001

Your ref. No.:_____

December 12th, 2007

Good Harvest Foodstuffs Co., LTD
234 Bay Street, Sydney
Australia

Attention: Manager of Imp. Dept.

Dear Sir,

Re: Invitation to Bid

Our corporation is willing to import from Australia various kinds of fruit jam including apple jam, pear jam, marmalade, pine-apple jam, apricot jam, strawberry jam and other Australian special jam.

Therefore your bids for the above products will be highly appreciated.

We are awaiting your early reply and thank you in advance.

Yours faithfully,
Tangjia
Tangjia
Shangwei Imp/Exp Corp.

Encl.: Our specifications requirements sheet

C.C.: Anderson& Son Company, Melbourne

P.S. Please attach the Copy Inspection Qualification certificates of yours products.

V. Put the following information into an envelope form:

写信人名称地址：Shaanxi Dragon University Imp/Exp Co., Ltd, Rms 1605-1611 Golden Eagle Mansion,10 Kepi Road, Xi'an Hi-tech Zone, Xi'an, Shaanxi, China 710068

收信人名称地址：Mr. Piyush Sharma, Shriram Global Minalloys Ltd. C-1, AMBABARI, JAIPUR-302023, INDIA

VI. Revise and improve the following letter:

Dear Sir,

We are importers of mailing machinery. We learnt from a friend that your new model RO-10 Mail Sorter is much more efficient. Your price remains the same.

Right now, the post offices of this country is undergoing a technical reform. There is a great demand for the machine.

We wish to place a trial order for two sets only. If your conditions are suitable, large orders will follow.

Please let us know your learns.

Please reply quickly.

Sincerely yours,
David

VII. Rearrange the sentences for clarity:

We are glad to say that we have found a ship which we think will serve you very well. The ship is now at Antwerp and can be ready to load at four or five days' definite notice. We thank you for your enquiry of May 9. The ship is Canilia with a cargo capacity of about 5,000 registered tons. And for a charter of 12 months the owners prepares to consider a special rate. We will prepare the charter party and send it to you as soon as we receive your cable confirmation.

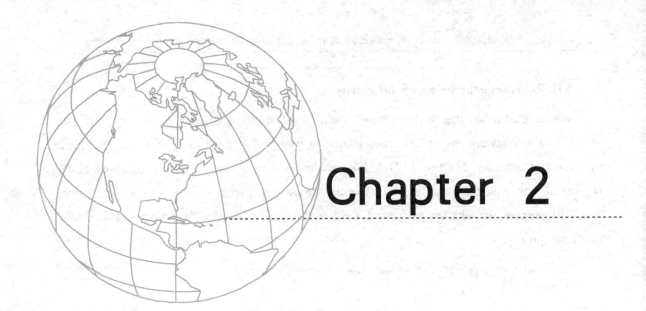

Chapter 2

Establishing Business Relations

Chapter 2 Establishing Business Relations

Task 1 Establishment of Business Relations

Part I. Introduction

The establishment of business relations means setting up business connections between two firms who have had no business dealings with each other before. Generally speaking, this type of letter begins by telling the addressee how his name is known. Then, some general information should be given as to the lines of business being handled. The writer should state simply, clearly and concisely what he can sell or what he expects to buy.

It is fairly true to say no customer, no business. To establish business relations with prospective dealers is the base of starting and developing of business. It is vitally important for both a new dealer and an old one that wish to enlarge its business scope and turnover.

If a new firm wishes to open up a market to sell something to or buy something from firms in foreign countries, the person in charge must first of all find out whom he is going to deal with. Usually, such information is obtainable through the following channels:

- Internet
- Banks
- Commercial Counselor's Office
- Chambers of Commerce both at home and abroad
- The introduction from his business connections or branches, agents aboard
- Advertisements
- Attendance at the export commodities fairs and exhibitions
- Mutual visits by trade delegations and groups
- Market investigations
- Self-introductions or enquiries received from the merchants abroad

Part II. Writing Skills

When writing letters to establish business relations, you should pay attention to the following steps:

Step 1: To state the source of customer's information (说明信息来源，从哪里知道对方).

Step 2: To introduce briefly one's own company (简短介绍自己所在公司).

Step 3: To express the purpose of writing the letter (表达写信的意图).

Step 4: To express the wish of business relations establishment and early reply (表达与对方建立业务关系的愿望及尽早收到对方回复的愿望).

Part III. Sample Letters

Sample 1   A letter from an Exporter

Dear sirs,

We have learnt from the Commercial Counselor's Office of the Chinese Embassy in Canada that you are in the market for Chinese garment products and now avail ourselves of this opportunity to approach you for entering into direct business relations with you.

As one of the leading exporters, we have been handling various kinds of Chinese leather products for about 10 years. Our products are very popular with many customers for their good quality and fine workmanship. To give you a general idea, we have sent you under separate cover several copies of illustrated catalogues and some sample cuttings.

Should any of the items be of interest to you, please let us know. We shall be glad to try our best to satisfy you at all times.

Yours faithfully,

China National Light Industrial Products Import and Export Corp.

Notes

1. We have learnt from the Commercial Counselor's Office of the Chinese Embassy in Canada that you are …

    我们从中国驻加拿大大使馆商务参赞处得知贵公司是……

    类似的表达方法还有：

    We owe your name and address to the chamber of commerce abroad.

    Through the courtesy of …, we learn your name and address.

    We are indebted to … for your name and address.

    We learn your name and address from…

2. be in the market for   想要购买，这一短语是外贸业务用语，与 wish to buy，want to buy 同义。

    e.g. We are in the market for black tea.   我们想要购买红茶.

3. avail ourselves of this opportunity to   利用这个机会

    e.g. We avail ourselves of this opportunity to thank you for your efforts in promoting the friendly business relations between us.   借此机会我们想感谢您为促进双方友好关系付出的努力。

Chapter 2 Establishing Business Relations

4. entering into 建立，开始（某种关系、事业、谈判）；缔结（契约等），与 establish 同义

5. leading exporters 主要出口商

6. good quality and fine workmanship 质量上乘，工艺精良

7. under separate cover 另函、另邮，与 send sth by separate mail 同义

   e.g. We shall send you samples under separate cover. 我们将另邮给您样品。

8. to give you a general idea 让你们大体了解

9. illustrated catalogues 附有插图的目录

Sample 2   A Letter from an Importer

NCE Trading Corporation
9 Alexander Street, London, England

July 23, 2009

China East Import.& Exp. Corporation.
Jiang Su, China
Tel:(025)8477889
Fax:(025)8477888

Gentlemen,

　　As your name and address were listed in the International Business Daily, we are writing in the hope of opening an account with your company.

　　We are one of the leading importers and wholesalers of various light industrial products in London, having a business background of some 40 years, and are now particularly interested in light industrial products of all types.

　　In order to let us have a better understanding of your products, would you please send us by return mail catalogues and prices of your products with full details. Upon receipt of such materials, we shall see what items are of interest to us and pass our enquiries to you.

　　If you need more objective information concerning our credit, please refer to the Midland Bank, London.

　　We anticipate the pleasure of hearing from you in the near future.

Truly yours,
David Lee

Notes

1. opening an account with your company 即 to enter into business relations with, 开立帐户。公司之间开帐户，意味着双方建立业务关系，等于 establish relations, 与……建立业务关系。

2. in the hope of 希望，"of" 后跟动名词

3. light industrial products 轻工业产品

4. let us have a better understanding of your products 让我们更好地了解产品

5. upon receipt of 收到

6. be of interest 感兴趣

   e.g. If you find any of our products are of interest to you, please let us know.
   如果你们对我们的任何产品感兴趣，请告知我方。

   If you find in our catalogue anything of interest, please let us know.
   如果商品目录中有你感兴趣的，请告知我方。

   Your new products are of interest to one of our customers.
   我们的一位客户对你方的新产品感兴趣。

7. refer to *vt.* 咨询、提交、查阅/*vi.* 谈到

8. anticipate 盼望，期待（其后用名词或动名词，不接不定式）

   e.g. We anticipate receiving your further orders.

Sample 3 Self-introduction by Exporter

Dear Sirs,

We write to introduce ourselves as one of the largest exporters, from China, of a wide range of Machinery and Equipments.

We enclose a copy of our latest catalogue covering the details of all the items that are available at present, and hope some of these items will be of interest to you.

It will be a great pleasure to receive your inquiries for any of the items against which we will send you our lowest quotation.

Should, by chance, your corporation not deal with the import of the goods mentioned above, we would be most grateful if this letter could be forwarded to the correct import corporation.

We are looking forward to your favorable and prompt reply.

Your faithfully,

(signature)

Notes

1. a wide range of… 大范围的……，各类的……

2. enclose *v.* 封入

    e.g. We enclose a copy of our price list. 随函附上我方价目表。

    enclosure *n.* 附件 缩写：Encl./Enc.

    enclose 和 attach 在汉语中都可翻译成"附着"，但这两个词在英语中的含义不同，enclose 的意思是"附在封套或信封内"，而 attach 则意为"附在某文件后"。因此，信函后的"附件"一般用 enclosure 一词，但强调某文件是随信而附时，则可用 attachment。

3. latest catalogue   最新目录

    catalogue for the standardized parts   标准化零件目录

    catalogue   目录

    pricelist   价格表，价目单

    literature   商业文字宣传品的统称，不可数名词，常有下面几种：

    　　manual   产品手册

    　　pamphlet (booklet, brochure)   小册子

    　　leaflet   单张说明书，广告单

    　　folder   折叠式印品

    　　bulletin   产品简报

    　　data   产品数据表

4. available *adj.* 可利用的，可得到的，可供应的（做定语时可前置，但后置较为常见）

    commodities available for export   供出口的商口

    not available   缺货

    e.g. We will ship by the first steamer available (or: the first available steamer) next month.
    　　货物将由下月第一条便船装运。

    　　This is the only stock available (or: the only available stock). 这是唯一可供之货。

    　　We are sending you under cover a catalog covering the goods available at present.
    　　随函附上一份我方目前可供货物的目录单。

5. inquiry *n.* 询价，询盘

6. quotation *n.* 报价，行情

    quotation list   价目表

market quotation   市场行情

quote   报价

quote a price   报价

7. deal with   经营、处理

e.g. Our company deals with the import and export of chemical products.

我们公司经营化工产品的进出口业务。

表示经营（某种或某类商品）的说法很多，常见的有：handle, deal in, trade in, be in the line of。

e.g. Our company handles the import and export of chemical products.

8. forward   *vt.* 转交，传递

9. favorable   *adj.* 有利的，赞成的，有帮助的，表示赞同某事或表示对某人、某事有利，后接介词 to

e.g. We are favorable to your terms and conditions of this transaction.

如果表示对某行为有利，一般接介词 for。

e.g. The time is not favorable for the disposal of the goods.

现在不是卖货的有利时机。

favorable reply   合意的回答、有利的答复，类似于 good news，相当于中文的"佳音"、"好消息"。

Task 2   Credit & Status Enquiries

Part I. Introduction

When you contact a company for business' sake for the first time, it is always important to get the necessary information about the company concerning 4 Cs (Credit, Character, Capital, Capacity), which means you should know about its reputation, financial status and business mode before conducting a transaction, especially the one that requires a large sum of money. Letters of requesting such information are called "credit and status inquiries".

There are several sources of the inquiries. You can obtain information either through the companies and banks that have business relations with the company under investigation or through inquiry agencies and chamber of commerce. The bank reference is objective and reliable but much simpler, lacking deeper understanding. Trade reference is more detailed but subjective. Usually, a bank will not give information about its clients unless the inquiries come from its fellow banks. For this reason, a bank reference should be demanded by the inquirer's own bank.

Chapter 2 Establishing Business Relations

Part II. Writing Skills

1. When writing letters of credit and status inquiries, you should pay attention to the following steps:

Step 1: Make sure your inquiry is handled by a third party that can be relied on, such as a bank, a chamber of commerce or another company.

Step 2: Briefly introduce the company to be inquired about.

Step 3: Make clear the relationship between the two parties and the reason for your inquiries.

Step 4: State the references on demand in details, such as financial standing, business scope and history of meeting obligations.

Step 5: Ensure that the information to be offered will be kept in the strictest secret.

Step 6: Inform that a stamped addressed envelope is enclosed.

Step 7: Express thanks and desire to get further help.

2. For answering letters of credit and status inquiries, the following should be paid more attention:

1. A letter of reply should be sincere and honest. Usually the word "confidential" is marked on the envelop.

2. The word "private and confidential" should be marked in the centre of the reply.

3. It is safer to use "the firm concerned", "the said firm" or "the firm in question" instead of mentioning the name especially when the reference report is discouraging or unfavorable.

4. Include such words as "this information is given without any responsibility" so as to avoid any possible trouble.

Part III. Sample Letters

Sample 1 An Inquiry about a Company

March 22, 2009

Dear Sirs,

　　As we are on the point of executing a considerable order from J.S. Husman Co., P.O. Box 386, Karachi, we should be much obliged if you would inform us, in confidence, of their financial standing and modes of business.

　　The reference they have given us is the Standard Chartered Bank, Karachi Branch. Will you please be good enough to approach the said bank for all possible information we require?

It goes without saying that any information you may obtain for us will be treated in the strictest confidence and you are free from any responsibility.

Yours faithfully,
Sales Manager

Notes

1. executing a considerable order　执行一份大宗订单

2. We should be much obliged if you would…　如果你们能……，我们将不胜感激。

3. financial standing　即 the reputation and status of finance，财务状况

4. business mode　即 the way of behaving in doing business，经营作风

5. in the strictest confidence　严格保密，与 in strict confidence 同义

Sample 2　A Favorable Reply

March 30, 2009

Dear Sirs,

　　In reply to your letter of March 22, we wish to inform you that we have now received from the Standard Chartered Bank, Karachi Branch, the information you required.

　　J.S. Husman Co., P.O. Box 386, Karachi, was established in 1979 with a capital of Stg 1000. They specialize in the import and export of machines and electrical equipments. Their suppliers' business with them is reported to have been satisfactory. We consider them good for small business engagement up to an amount of Stg. 3000. For large transactions we suggest payment by sight L/C.

　　The above information is strictly confidential and given without any responsibility on this bank.

Yours faithfully,
(signature)

Notes

1. in reply to　兹回复

2. specialize in　专门经营

3. up to　直到，相当于，胜任，该由……决定

4. sight L/C　即 sight letter of credit，即期付款信用证

Chapter 2　Establishing Business Relations

Sample 3　An Unfavorable Reply

> March 30, 2009
>
> Dear Sirs,
>
> 　　Upon receipt of your letter of March 22, we made inquiries concerning the firm you mentioned and have obtained the following information:
>
> 　　The mentioned firm is known to be heavily committed and have overrun their reserves. They are being pressed by several creditors and their position is precarious. It would, therefore, appear inadvisable to enter into any credit transaction with this firm.
>
> 　　Please consider this information as given in strict confidence.
>
> 　　　　　　　　　　　　　　　　　　　　Yours faithfully,
> 　　　　　　　　　　　　　　　　　　　　　(signature)

Notes

1. upon receipt of　收到
2. heavily committed　大量承约
3. overrun　超越
4. precarious　*adj*. 不确定的，危险的
5. inadvisable　*adj*. 不受劝告的，不聪明的，不得体的
6. credit transaction　即 credit business，信用交易

Part IV.　Useful Expressions and Typical Sentences

Useful Expressions

1. enjoy a high reputation　享有很高声誉

2. We owe your name and address to...

承蒙……，我们得知贵公司的名称和地址。

类似的表达方法有：

Through the courtesy of…, we learn your name and address.

We are indebted to… for your name and address.

We learn your name and address from…

On recommendation of …Co. ltd, we have learned with pleasure the name of your firm and shall be glad to enter into business relations with you.

3. deal exclusively in　独家经营

4. sole agency   独家代理

5. chain store   连锁商店

6. avail oneself of   利用

7. refer sb. to   引……去查询

8. credit and financial standing   公司的信贷债务信誉和财务状况

9. favorable balance of trade   贸易顺差

10. the Commercial Counselor's Office   商务参赞处

11. the chamber of commerce   商会

12. specialize in   专门经营

13. cotton piece goods   棉织品，棉布

14. excellent in quality and reasonable in price   品质优良，价格合理

15. a state-operated/ owned/ run corporation   国营公司

16. one of the leading exporters   主要出口商之一

17. be in the market for   想要购买

18. enter into business relations   建立贸易关系

19. a well-established exporter   信誉良好的出口商

20. fall within the scope of our business activities   属于我方经营范围

Typical Sentences

1. We owe your name and address to the chamber of commerce abroad.

2. Enclosed please find a copy of our pricelist. / Please find enclosed a copy of our pricelist.

3. We have the pleasure to introduce ourselves to you with a view to building up business relations with your firm.

4. Specializing in the export of Chinese Cotton Piece Goods, we express our desire to trade with you in this line.

5. Please submit full specifications of your products together with terms of payment and discount rate.

6. In order to give you some idea of various qualities of handicrafts we carry, we have pleasure in forwarding you by air one catalogue.

7. Our banks are the Hong Kong & Shanghai banking Corporation in Hong Kong, they can provide you with the information about our business and finances.

8. We should be pleased /highly appreciate it if you would respond to our request at your earliest convenience.

9. We are willing to establish business relations with your corporation on the basis of equality, mutual benefit and supplying each other's needs.

Chapter 2 Establishing Business Relations

10. You are introduced to us by Johnson Co., Ltd. as one of the leading importers of electronic products.

11. We write to introduce ourselves as exporters of Health Tea having 30 years' experience in this line of business.

12. It will be to our mutual benefit to develop business between us.

13. We would like you to inquire into the financial and credit status of a firm in Milan on our behalf.

14. You are kindly requested to provide us with the information about credit and business operation of Smith Import Company.

15. Please be convinced that all the materials you supply to us will be kept in absolute secret, for which you will not take any responsibilities.

16. In the local business community he is regarded as a substantial trader with a clean record.

17. The foregoing information is given in confidence and for your private use only and this bank or its officials are free from any responsibility.

18. In reply to your inquiry of September 26 concerning the firm in question, we would recommend a policy of caution.

19. We hardly need to say that any information you give us will be used in complete confidence.

20. The firm you inquired about has always met its commitments satisfactorily.

Part V. Project Training

Project 1

Training Situation:

China Textile Imp. & Exp. Corporation, Jiangsu Branch has handled garments for more than twenty years. Their products are well known in the world market and they want to establish direct business relations with H.W. Wallace & Co. 194 St. Louis Street Corydon, England.

Training Requirements:

The students are required to write a letter to the foreign importer, and the letter should cover at least the following points:
- the information about the foreign company
- the desire
- the business scope

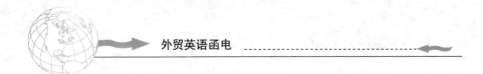

Project 2

Training Situation:

China National Textiles Import & Export Corp. mainly deals in textiles products which enjoys great popularity in the world. He gets the name and address of ABC Co. in Australia from the Chamber of Commerce in this country.

Training Requirements:

Practise writing a letter to ABC Co. to express the wish of establishing business relations.

Hints:

- the objectives
- the information about the ABC Co.

Project 3

Training Situation:

China Trading Company Ltd. is going to import electronic equipments from the Global Trading Co. P.O. Box 3241, San Francisco, California, U.S.A. They haven't known each other before.

Training Requirements:

The students are required to write a letter to the exporter.

Hints:

- Commercial Counselor's Office
- dealing with electronic products
- the reference as to the company's financial standing
- The students may add a Subject Line for the letter

Project 4

Training Situation:

Mr. Burgers, manager of Messrs. B. T. Greenwood & Co. 315 Manor St., London E14 8PH, England, wants to import some Chinese cotton piece goods. He has learned the name and address of China National Silks Import & Export Corporation from Messrs. Hussain & Co., P. O. Box 386, Karachi.

Training Requirements:

According to the given information, students should be divided into two groups, one acts as importer, the other as exporter, and do as the following instructions:
- Write a letter to exporter for establishment of business relations
- Write a letter to a bank, asking for all possible information about the importer
- Make a dialogue according to the situation

Part VI. Optional Study

I. Related Information

ICC (International Chamber of Commerce) is the voice of world business championing the global economy as a force for economic growth, job creation and prosperity.

Because national economies are now so closely interwoven, government decisions have far stronger international repercussions than in the past.

ICC—the world's only truly global business organization responds by being more assertive in expressing business views.

ICC activities cover a broad spectrum, from arbitration and dispute resolution to making the case for open trade and the market economy system, business self-regulation, fighting corruption or combating commercial crime.

ICC has direct access to national governments all over the world through its national committees. The organization's Paris-based international secretariat feeds business views into intergovernmental organizations on issues that directly affect business operations.

Setting Rules and Standards

Arbitration under the rules of the ICC International Court of Arbitration is on the increase. Since 1999, the Court has received new cases at a rate of more than 500 a year.

ICC's Uniform Customs and Practice for Documentary Credits (UCP 500) are the rules that banks apply to finance billions of dollars worth of world trade every year.

ICC Inco terms are standard international trade definitions used every day in countless thousands of contracts. ICC model contracts make life easier for small companies that cannot afford big legal departments.

ICC is a pioneer in business self-regulation of e-commerce. ICC codes on advertising and marketing are frequently reflected in national legislation and the codes of professional associations.

Promoting Growth and Prosperity

ICC supports government efforts to make a success of the Doha trade round. ICC provides world business recommendations to the World Trade Organization.

ICC speaks for world business when governments take up such issues as intellectual property rights, transport policy, trade law or the environment.

Signed articles by ICC leaders in major newspapers and radio and TV interviews reinforce the ICC stance on trade, investment and other business topics.

Every year, the ICC Presidency meets with the leader of the G8 host country to provide business input to the summit.

ICC is the main business partner of the United Nations and its agencies.

Spreading Business Expertise

At UN summits on sustainable development, financing for development and the information society, ICC spearheads the business contribution.

Together with the United Nations Conference on Trade and Development (UNCTAD), ICC helps some of the world's poorest countries to attract foreign direct investment.

In partnership with UNCTAD, ICC has set up an Investment Advisory Council for the least-developed countries.

ICC mobilizes business support for the New Partnership for Africa's Development. At ICC World Congresses every two years, business executives tackle the most urgent international economic issues.

The World Chambers Congress, also biennial, provides a global forum for chambers of commerce.

Regular ICC regional conferences focus on the concerns of business in Africa, Asia, the Arab World and Latin America.

Advocate for International Business

ICC speaks for world business whenever governments make decisions that crucially affect corporate strategies and the bottom line.

ICC's advocacy has never been more relevant to the interests of thousands of member companies and business associations in every part of the world.

Equally vital is ICC's role in forging internationally agreed rules and standards that companies adopt voluntarily and can be incorporated in binding contracts.

Chapter 2　Establishing Business Relations

ICC provides business input to the United Nations, the World Trade Organization, and many other intergovernmental bodies, both international and regional.

II. Supplementary Specimen Letters

Specimen Letter 1   Asking to Establish Business Relations

Dear Sirs,

　　Through the courtesy of the Commercial Counselor's Office of your embassy in Beijing, we have known that you are importers of Cotton Piece Goods and interested in doing business with us. We wish to inform you that we specialize in the export of Cotton Piece Goods and shall be pleased to establish business relations with you at an early date.

　　Chinese Cotton Piece Goods are excellent in quality and reasonable in price. To give you a general idea of our products, we are sending you under separate cover a catalogue together with three pamphlets for your information. We shall be pleased to give you a quotation upon receipt of your specific inquires.

　　We look forward to hearing from you soon.

Yours faithfully,

(signature)

Specimen Letter 2   Manufacturer Writes to Importer

Dear Sirs,

　　We owe your name and address to the Chamber of Commerce, Tokyo, who has informed us that you are in the market for Personal Computers.

　　We are one of the largest computer manufacturers in our country and have handled the products for about 10 years. We approach you today in the hope of establishing business relations with you and expect, by our joint efforts, to enlarge our business scope.

　　In order to acquaint you with our business lines, we enclose a copy of our illustrated catalogue covering the main items sup pliable at present. If you are interested in any of the items, please tell us by fax. We'll give you our lowest quotations and try our best to comply with your requirement.

　　Our customers are always satisfied with our products and the service after selling. And we believe that you will be satisfied too, after we do business together.

　　Our banks are Bank of Tokyo, Japan. They can provide you information about our business and finances.

We are looking forward to your early reply.

Yours faithfully,
(signature)

Specimen Letter 3   Credit Status Inquiry

Dear Sirs,

Recently we have received an order amounting to the value of USD 150000 from a new customer—the Colston Engineering Company, Ltd., in Lagos, Nigeria. As we have never done any business with them before, we wonder if you could obtain for us information about their financial and credit standing. Their reference is the National Bank of Nigeria, Logos.

Any information you may give us will be treated strictly in confidence.

Thank you in advance for you cooperation.

Yours faithfully,
Shanghai Art ware Import & Export Corporation

Specimen Letter 4   A Reply to Credit Standing Inquiry

Dear Sirs,

We have received from the National Bank of Nigeria, Lagos the information regarding the Colston Engineering Company, Ltd. and regret that we must advise you to proceed with every possible caution in your dealing with them.

The company in question is a private company run by two brothers. Suppliers often have lots of trouble in settlement of their accounts. About a year ago an action was brought against them by one of their suppliers for recovery of the sums due though payment was recovered in full.

In view of their position, you are suggested to do business with them on L/C or cash basis.

This information is of course supplied in the strictest confidence and without any responsibility on our part.

Yours faithfully,
Information Service Dept.
Bank of China, Shanghai Branch

Chapter 2 Establishing Business Relations

Part VII. Exercises

I. Translate the following terms and expressions:

A. Into Chinese:

1. leading exporter
2. light industrial products
3. market quotation
4. execute a considerable order
5. reply to
6. credit transaction
7. lowest quotation
8. comply with one's requirement
9. financial and credit standing
10. in the strictest confidence

B. Into English:

1. 建立业务关系
2. 产品目录
3. 专门经营
4. 执行订单
5. 收到
6. 大量承约
7. 财务状况
8. 供出口的商品
9. 在……行业
10. 最新目录

II. Choose the best answer to complete each of the following sentences:

1. We hope to enter_____ business relations_____ your firm.
   A. into; with   B. with; into   C. /;at   D. in; in
2. We are sending you the samples_____ requested.
   A. be   B. are   C. as   D. for
3. We are _____ a copy of our catalog for your reference.
   A. send   B. covering   C. closed   D. enclosing
4. We would like to take this_____ to establish business relations with you.
   A. opening   B. opportunity   C. step   D. advantage
5. If any of the items is _____to you, please let us know.
   A. interest   B. interesting   C. interested   D. interests
6. We assure you _____our best service _____any time.
   A. for; in   B. at; on   C. of; at   D. with; at
7. Please quote us your_____ price on CFR basis.
   A .lower possible   B. possible low   C. lowest possible   D. possible lowest

8. _____ recommendation of ABC Co., we have learned that you are _____ the market _____ "Meiling" brand canned goods.

    A. At; on; of   B. Upon; in; of   C. On; in; for   D. In; at; for

9. We will send you a complete range of samples _____ your reply.

    A. upon receipt of   B. upon the receipt of

    C. on the receipt of   D. till receipt of

10. As the item _____ the scope of our business activities, we shall be pleased to establish trade relations with you.

    A. lies within   B. fall within   C. come under   D. be within

III. Supply the missing words in the blanks of the following letters. The first letters are given:

Letter A

Dear Sirs,

    We have l_____ from the Commercial Counselor's Office of our Embassy in your country that you are in the m_____ for Chinese electronic products.

    We i_____ ourselves as well-established e_____ of all kinds of Chinese goods, especially of Electronic and Hi-fi products. And we would l_____ to enter i_____ business relations with you.

    Our products are of high q_____ and r_____ price, and have long e_____ a great fame at home and a_____. We enclose a c_____ for your i_____ and t_____ some of the items will be of _____ to you.

    We look forward to your e_____ reply.

                                                            Yours faithfully,

                                                                     (signature)

Letter B

Dear Sirs,

    We have h_____ from the Chamber of Commerce i_____ Japan that you are o_____ of the leading importers of textiles in _____ your country. As this items f_____ within the s_____ of our business activities, we hope to e_____ business relations w_____ you. In order t_____ give you a general idea of our products, we e_____

Chapter 2　Establishing Business Relations

here with a catalogue and a price list. Quotations and samples will be s_____ upon r_____ of your specific e_____.

　　We shall be p_____ to hear from you a _____ your earliest convenience.

Yours　faithfully,
(signature)

IV. Translate the following sentences into English:

1．我们想与你公司建立业务关系。

2．我们是一家专门经营自行车进出口的国有公司。

3．我们已经向你方另封寄出我们全部产品的目录清单。

4．我们的一个客户想要购买中国红茶。

5．从阿里巴巴网站上获悉贵方有意购买中国绿茶，我公司经营茶叶已十余年，很愿意与贵方建立相互之间的业务关系。

V. Write a letter with the following particulars:

1．经你方商会的介绍，我方欣悉贵公司的行名和地址。

2．我公司专门经营中国纺织品出口，并愿意在平等互利的基础上与贵公司建立业务关系。

3．为使贵方对我方产品有全面的了解，我方另函寄去一本目录册及一套小册子以供参考。

4．如对目录中所列之任何产品感兴趣，请具体询价，我方将立即报价。

5．期待早日回复。

Chapter 3

Enquiry and Reply

Chapter 3 Enquiry and Reply

Task 1 Making an Enquiry

Part I. Introduction

Enquiry is the first step after the establishment of business. When an importer wants to import something, he may send an enquiry to the exporter. An enquiry is made to seek a supply of products, service or information. In order to obtain the needed information, the enquirer should state simply, clearly and concisely what he wants—general information, a catalogue or a price list, a sample, a quotation, etc. Enquiries should be specific and provide the necessary details to enable the receiver to answer the questions completely. There are two types of enquiry, one is a general enquiry, and the other is a specific enquiry. General enquiries ask for common data, such as catalogue, price list, sample and pictures, etc. Specific enquiries specifically enquire about name of commodity, specifications, quantity, unit price, date of shipment, payment terms and packing, etc.

Part II. Writing Skills

Write a letter of enquiry:

1. Letters of inquiry normally consist of the following parts:
   - introducing yourself and where you heard about the product or company
   - explaining why you are writing
   - listing the specific information you need in the form of detailed questions
   - closing your letter with appreciation and a request for an early reply

2. Give the source from which you learned about the company or the product.

   e.g. I read about your product in China Daily of March 13.

   I heard about your product from a friend who has used it.

   We refer to your advertisement in the latest issue of The International Trade News.

3. Be specific about what you want so as to make it easy for recipient to identify and provide the information you need.

   e.g. We are interested in discussing arts and crafts business with you.

   I want to purchase some chinaware from your company.

   We are very much interested in Hangzhou printed pure silk fabrics.

4. Ask for information about your specific needs, e.g., the price, availability, different models or styles, the delivery date, the mode of shipping.

e.g. We are thinking of placing an order for MTC-26.

What is the distinguishing feature of the Model 612 motorcycle?

Please quote for the supply of 3000 metric tons of steel pipes.

Please quote us the lowest prices CIFC5 Rotterdam and indicate the quantities and sizes respectively that you can supply for prompt shipment.

5. Emphasize the value of the wanted information to you. Offer your reader some incentive for responding.

e.g. We are evaluating your product to see if it will be beneficial to our company.

We are hoping that your product will be able to save us money.

As we are likely to place large orders regularly we trust you will consider the allowance of some special concessions.

6. Make the tone of the letter friendly and courteous by saying "please", "I would appreciate", "thank you", etc.

e.g. Thank you for your assistance and early response.

We thank you in advance for sending the catalog and price list.

Part III. Sample Letters

Sample 1   A General Inquiry

United Textiles Ltd.

York House, Lawton Street

Liverpool, ML3 2LL

England

Tel: ...   Fax: ...   E-mail: ...

Our Ref: CT-GZ

Your Ref:

September 16, 2007

Guangdong Textiles Import & Export Corporation

779 East Dongfeng Road

Guangzhou

China

Dear Sirs,

   Messrs. Brown & Clark of this city inform us that you are an exporter of all kinds of cotton bed sheets and pillowcases. We would like you to send us details of your various

Chapter 3 Enquiry and Reply

ranges, including sizes, colors and prices, and also samples of the different qualities of material used.

  We are one of the largest dealers in textiles and believe there is a promising market in our area for moderately priced goods of the kind mentioned.

  Looking forward to your early reply.

Yours faithfully,
United Textiles Ltd.
Manager

Notes

1. dealer   经销商

2. promising market   有前景的市场

3. moderately   适度地，合适地

Sample 2   A Specific Inquiry

The Elegant Leather Product Inc.

9 Green Street

Manchester

England

Tel:

Fax:

22 March 2004

Granford Leather Stores

22 Western Highway

New York

USA

Dear Sir,

  We have learned from Messrs. Armstrong & Smith of Liverpool that you manufacture a range of high-fashion handbags in a variety of leathers. As we are one of the leading dealers of leather handbags in this area and believe there is a promising market here for handbags of high quality, we would like you to send us details of your various ranges, including sizes, colors and prices, and also samples of the different qualities of skins used.

When replying, please state your terms of payment and discount you would allow on purchases of large quantities of individual items. Prices quoted should include insurance and freight to Liverpool.

Should prices be found reasonable and suitable for our market, we shall be pleased to place regular order with you.

We hope that will meet your prompt attention.

Yours sincerely,

(signature)

Notes

1. terms of payment   支付方式

2. insurance and freight   保险费和运费

3. place regular order with sb.   向某人定期订购

Task 2　Reply to an Enquiry

Part I. Introduction

Reply letters answer questions, supply information and/or materials, offer special help and attempt to satisfy the needs of those who make the requests.

Replies to letters of inquiry should be prompt. You are expected to respond within two days except for some special reasons. In that case, you should inform the customer in advance so as to make the customer feel they are valued.

Part II. Writing Skills

Write a letter of reply to an enquiry:

1. All replies start with an acknowledgement of the inquiry, restating the date and the request.

e.g. We are very pleased to receive your letter of October 3.

　　Thank you for your inquiry of June 5 for our Word Processor AW100.

　　We are happy to receive your letter of October 30 requesting a catalog of our product.

2. The middle paragraph provides clear and comprehensive answers to the inquiry. You can also provide additional information to the questions related but not asked.

e.g. As requested, we have today sent you two copies of our latest catalogs by separate airmail.

　　We are pleased to send you samples of our products with their quotations and discount.

Of the samples we sent you, we believe No.5 will suit your need best.

3. The last paragraph expresses the hope that the information will be of help and the hope for an immediate reply.

e.g. We thank you for your interest in our products and wait for your early reply.

An order you might give us will receive our careful attention.

We look forward to the opportunity of being of service to you soon.

Please contact us for any questions.

4. If you are unable to supply goods or service requested, give explanation and apology.

e.g. We regret that the goods you inquired about are not available.

The goods you inquired about are not available at the price you specified.

I am sorry this is out of stock.

5. When enclosing additional materials like brochures, prices lists, etc. mention the enclosure generally rather than explain every item in them.

Part III. Sample Letters

Sample 1 A Reply to the General Enquiry

Guangdong Textiles Import & Export Corporation
779 East Dongfeng Road
Guangzhou, China
Tel: ...   Fax: ...   E-mail: ...
Our Ref: GD 2007 (8)
Your Ref: CT-GZ
September 22, 2007
United Textiles Ltd.
York House, Lawton Street
Liverpool, ML3 2LL
England
Dear Sirs,

    We are very pleased to receive your inquiry of September 16 and enclose our illustrated catalogue and price list giving the details you ask for. Also by separate post we are sending you some samples and feel confident that when you have examined them you will agree that the goods are both excellent in quality and reasonable in price.

    We also invite your attention to our other products such as table-cloths and table napkins, details of which you will find in the catalogue, and look forward to receiving your first order.

>   Yours sincerely,
>   Guangdong Textiles Import & Export Corporation
>   Manager

Notes

by separate post   另封邮寄

Sample 2   A Reply to the Specific Enquiry

Granford Leather Stores
22 Western Highway
New York
USA
Tel:
Fax:
The Elegant Leather Product Inc.
9 Green Street
Manchester
England
Dear Sirs,

　　We are very pleased to receive your enquiry of 22 March and hear that you are interested in our products.

　　We are sending you our illustrated catalogue and price list under separate cover, together with samples of some of the skins we regularly use in the manufacture of the products. You may rest assured that the quality of materials used and high standard of craftsmanship will appeal to the most selective buyer. On regular purchases in quantities of not less than 100 dozen of individual items we would allow you a discount of 3%. Payment is to be made by irrevocable L/C at sight.

　　We also manufacture a wide range of leather gloves and wallets in which you may be interested. They are fully illustrated in our catalogue and are of the same high quality as our handbags.

　　We look forward to receiving an order from you.

                                                              Yours truly,
                                                              (signature)

Chapter 3 Enquiry and Reply

Notes

1. illustrated catalogue   带有插图的产品目录
2. under separate cover / by separate mail   另函，另封，另寄
    e.g. We are sending you catalogues under separate cover / by separate mail.
3. rest assured / be assured   确信
4. irrevocable L/C at sight   不可撤销的即期信用证
5. selective buyers   挑剔的买主，有眼力的买家

Part IV. Useful Expressions and Typical Sentences

Useful Expressions

1. take/have/feel/be interest in...   对……感兴趣
2. be in the market for..., be desirous of..., desire   想购买……，想要……
3. make/send sb. an inquiry for..., inquire (for)...   询购……
4. illustrated catalogue   带有图片说明的目录表
5. Please state terms of...   请说明……的条款。
6. This is in reply to one's inquiry of...   兹答复某人……的询盘。
7. date of delivery   交货期
8. lowest/best price   最低价；favorable price   最优惠价；
    rock-bottom price   底价；competitive price   竞争价；reasonable price   合理价
9. place an order with sb. for sth.   向某人订购某物
10. regular order   定期购买；regular supply   定期供应
11. special discount   特别折扣
12. bulk buying   大量购买
13. available from stock   有存货的
14. make/cable sb. an offer for...   就……商品给某人报盘；给……报盘
15. up-to-date/latest price list   最新价目表
16. as specified below   下列
17. steady demand   稳定的需求
18. ready market   现成的市场；成熟的市场
19. the taste of the market   市场需求/品味/偏好
20. be under offer, be on sale   （商品）在出售中

45

Typical Sentences

1. Will you please send us your illustrated/latest catalogue and full details of your prices and terms of payment, together with samples?

2. Please send me a copy of your description of the electric hedge trimmers.

3. We would be pleased if you send us your lowest quotation for the following.

4. A client of ours is interested in securing a certain quantity of Chinese Cotton Piece Goods, as specified below, for which you are requested to make an offer.

5. We have pleasure in informing you that we are interested in your plastic kitchenware and would like you to make us an offer.

6. We have an inquiry in hand for a large quantity of Bitter Apricot Kernels.

7. We understand that there is a good demand for glassware in your market, and take this opportunity of enclosing our quotation No.1338 for your consideration.

8. We are sending you by airmail a small sample. A copy of the relative description leaflet is enclosed.

9. Will you please send us your catalogue together with a detailed offer?

10. Please inform us of the prices of the products that you can supply.

11. We'd like to have your lowest quotations CIF Vancouver.

12. We have seen your advertisement in China's Foreign Trade and would be glad if you will send us the particulars of bed sheets and pillowcases.

13. You must take into consideration when quoting a price that we may place regular orders for large quantities.

14. Kindly let us know the prices and quantities of the best refined sugar you are able to deliver to us.

15. We have ready buyers of these commodities and if your prices are competitive, we have every reason to believe that we can place large orders with you.

16. We would be pleased if you would let us have a list of items that are exported by you.

17. We have an importer inquiring for woolen blankets and would like to obtain a catalogue and price list together with the samples as soon as possible.

18. We would be much obliged if you could quote us the best CIFC5 Shanghai and indicate the respective quantities and various sizes that you could supply for prompt shipment.

19. Please let us know on what terms you can supply the above goods.

20. If you are in a position to meet our demand, we will place a large order with you.

Chapter 3 Enquiry and Reply

Part V. Project Training

Project 1

Training Situation:

Thomas Co. Ltd. is one of the leading importers of handicraft articles in Canada, and is now in the market for high quality brocade handbags. They learned from the Commercial Counselor's Office of Canadian Embassy that Ningbo Qianhu Trading Co. Ltd. was in abundant supply of brocade handbags. So Mr. Martin Crown in the Purchasing department of Thomas Co. Ltd. makes contact with Ningbo Qianhu Trading Co. Ltd. and makes an enquiry about its brocade handbags.

Training Requirements:

Student A: Write a letter of enquiry in the name of Martin Crown.

Student B: Write a letter of reply to Martin Crown in the name of Mr. Chen in the Export Department of Ningbo Qianhu Trading Co. Ltd.

Project 2

Training Situation:

You work for Wihan Tea I/E Corp, 45 Wenhua Road, Wuhan 200450. You have received a letter of enquiry about tea from Miracle Trading Company, England.

Training Requirements:

Write a letter of reply. The following points must be included:

1. thanks for enquiry
2. enclose a latest catalogue and price list
3. introduce some other products
4. for further information, please fax or telephone us
5. expect to receive orders

Part VI. Optional study

I. Related Information

1. Enquiries mean potential business. Prompt and careful replies are of great importance.

2. When making enquiries, give details of your own firm and ask for needed information from your prospective supplier. Be specific and state exactly what you want: the goods needed,

usual terms of trade, a catalogue, a price list, a sample, a quotation, etc., so as to enable the seller to quote or offer the correct goods.

3. The tactic often used to invite better terms is to give the seller some hope of substantial orders or continued business.

4. In an enquiry such phrases are often used as "Should your prices be competitive", "If your quotation is favorable" or "Please quote your best prices".

5. When giving replies to enquiries, make sure that you have answered all the customer's questions, and include all the points you want to make, assure your customer that you have faith in your product or service, which means that you have to "sell" it.

II. Supplementary Specimen Letters

Specimen Letter 1

China National Textile Imp. & Exp. Corp.

No. 82, Dong'anmennei Street

Beijing, China

Dear Sirs,

  We have noticed from your advertisement in "China Export Directory" that you export large quantities of Chinese acrylic blankets to our neighboring countries each year and would like to know whether you can supply us on CFR basis.

  Being Specialized in this line, we are experienced and well connected with many customers in our country. Various kinds of blankets can find a good market here, especially those fine in quality but low in price. We shall be grateful if you will send us some brochures and samples for our reference.

  If the goods and your trade terms prove satisfactory, you may expect from us substantial orders in the future.

Yours faithfully,
Allen Incorporation

Notes

1. China Export Directory   中国出口指南

2. acrylic blanket   晴纶毯

3. be well connected with sb.   与某人关系好，与某人关系密切

  e.g. We wonder if you are well connected with the local suppliers.

Chapter 3 Enquiry and Reply

4. a good market   畅销，好销路

    e.g. Garments of good quality and attractive design can enjoy a good market everywhere.

5. for one's reference   供某人参考

6. trade terms   交易条款

7. substantial   大量的，多的

    e.g. We have received substantial enquiries for Bicycle Model 18.

Specimen Letter 2

Ningbo Qianhu Trading Co., Ltd.
101 Lianfeng Road
Ningbo 315000
China

Dear Sirs,

　　We have learned from the Commercial Counselor's Office of Canadian Embassy in your country that you manufacture and export a variety of handicraft articles.

　　Our company is one of the leading importers of handicraft articles in Canada. As there is a steady demand here for high quality brocade handbags, we would like you to send us as soon as possible your illustrated catalogues, samples and all necessary information about the goods. Meanwhile, please quote your lowest price, CIF Vancouver, stating the earliest date of shipment.

　　Should your quality be suitable and the price competitive, we'll be ready to place an order for at least 5,000 pieces with you.

　　Your prompt attention to this matter will be much appreciated.

Yours faithfully,
Martin Crown

Notes

1. the Commercial Counselor's Office of Canadian Embassy in your country   加拿大驻贵国大使馆商务参赞处

2. illustrated catalogue   带插图的商品目录

3. quote … lowest price   报最低价

4. date of shipment   装运日期

Specimen Letter 3

Bradley & Bros Plc.

18 West Way, Runcorne

Cheshire, U.K.

Tel: ...   Fax: ...   E-mail: ...

Our Ref:

Your Ref:

August 8, 2007

Guangdong Light Industries Products Import & Export Corporation

779 East Dongfeng Road

Guangzhou, P. R. China

Dear Madam or Sir,

    We have noticed from your advertisement in www.chinaproducts.com.cn that you export large quantities of cushions to European markets.

    Being specialized in this line for a long time, we are well connected with many customers in our country. At present, we are interested in back cushions fine in quality and low in price. It would be highly appreciated if you could send us some brochures and samples for our reference and quote your lowest price on CIF basis including our 3% commission.

    Should your goods prove satisfactory and the price be found competitive, you may expect substantial orders from us. We are looking forward to your early reply.

                                                      Yours faithfully,

                                                      Jean Bean

                                                       Manager

Notes

1. www.chinaproducts.com.cn   中国出口商品网

2. cushion   *n.* 垫子，软垫

   back cushions   靠背垫

3. be well connected with   与某人关系好，与某人联系密切

   e.g. We think you are well connected with the local buyers.

Chapter 3 Enquiry and Reply

Specimen Letter 4

Guangdong Light Industries Products Import & Export Corporation

779 East Dongfeng Road

Guangzhou, P. R. China

Tel: ...   Fax: ...   E-mail: ...

Our Ref:

Your Ref:

August 15, 2007

Mr. Jean Bean

Manager

Bradley & Bros Plc.

18 West Way, Runcorne

Cheshire, U.K.

Dear Mr. Bean,

　　Your inquiry of August 8, 2007, has been well received. Thank you very much for your interest in our cushions.

　　We are enclosing samples and a price list of back cushions giving the details you asked for. We feel confident that you will find the goods both excellent in quality and reasonable in price.

Yours sincerely,

Ms. Wang

Sales Manager

Encls: as stated

Notes

1. excellent in quality and reasonable in price   质量上乘，价格合理

2. Encls: as stated   附件如上所述

Part VII. Exercises

I. Translate the following terms and expressions:

A: Into Chinese:

1. illustrated catalogue   2. date of delivery

3. special discount
4. the taste of the market
5. up-to-date/latest price list
6. promising market
7. bulk buying
8. available from stock
9. as specified below
10. be under offer, be on sale

B: Into English:

1. 询价单
2. 另封邮寄
3. 想购买……，想要……
4. 不可撤销的即期信用证
5. 最低价/最优惠价
6. 询购
7. 兹答复某人……的询盘
8. 向某人订购某物
9. 现成的市场，成熟的市场
10. 请说明……的条款

II. Choose the best answer to complete each of the following sentences:

1. Please let us have details of your machine tools, _____ your earliest delivery.
   A. giving us   B. give us   C. to give us   D. given us

2. We hope to receive your quotation with details _____ the possible time of shipment.
   A. to include   B. to be included   C. including   D. being included

3. Will you please send us your price lists for the items _____ below.
   A. listing   B. being listed   C. to list   D. listed

4. We shall appreciate _____ us FOB Sydney.
   A. you quoting   B. your quoting   C. you to quote   D. your being quoted

5. If you can supply your goods immediately, we shall _____ to place a prompt trial order.
   A. be prepared   B. be preparing   C. prepare   D. preparing

6. As we have an extensive business connection in this field, we hope_____ your special terms.
   A. to give   B. giving   C. to be given   D. to be giving

7. If your prices are competitive, we are confident _____ the goods in great quantities in this market.
   A. to sell   B. to be selling   C. in being sold   D. in selling

8. We confirm our cable just dispatched _____ the following items.
   A. offering you firm   B. firm offering you
   C. to be offered to you firm   D. to firm offer you

9. We offer you the following items _____ your reply reaching here by 3 p.m. April 12, our time.

    A. subjecting to   B. to subject to

    C. subjects to   D. subject to

10. This offer is _____ your acceptance by cable on or before October 11.

    A. effective to   B. effectively for

    C. effective for   D. effectively to

11. A comparison of your offer _____ our regular suppliers shows that their terms are more favorable.

    A. with what of   B. with those of

    C. with which of   D. with these of

12. We certainly accept your offer _____ you will ship the goods during August.

    A. except   B. provided   C. unless   D. but

13. _____ you make a 10% reduction, we will have to decline your offer this time.

    A. When   B. Except   C. As   D. Unless

14. As we are one of the leading importers in this line, we are _____ a position to handle large quantities.

    A. at   B. in   C. on   D. of

15. Although we appreciate the good quality of your goods, we are sorry to say that your price appears to be _____.

    A. of the high standards   B. in the high level

    C. on the high side   D. at the high

III. Translate the following sentences into Chinese:

1. One of our customers takes interest in the model 123, and we would like to receive a sample and quotation.

2. I'm interested in your Green Tea. I think some of the items will find a ready market at our end. I'd like to have your lowest quotation CIF Victoria.

3. We are in the market for men's shirts illustrated in your catalogue No.4. Please quote us your lowest price with the best discount and the date of delivery.

4. Please quote your lowest price CIF Singapore for each of the following items, inclusive of our 3% commission.

5. We hope that your prices will be workable and that business will result to our mutual benefit.

6. We have seen your advertisement in the *Overseas Journal* and would be glad to have price list and details of your terms.

7. We understand that you are manufacturers of air conditioners and would like to know whether you can supply the items as specified below.

8. Enclosed: please find samples of our Nylon Socks. If you are able to supply us with 5000 dozen, we would be pleased to have you quote a favorable price CIF Hong Kong.

9. The articles we require are listed on the attached sheet. If you have them in stock, please tell us the quantity and also the lowest CIF Hong Kong price.

10. Some of our customers have an interest in your canned goods and we wish to have your CIF quotations with samples and full particulars.

IV. Translate the following sentences into English:

1. 我们拟购男式皮手套，请报最优惠价格为荷。

2. 请用传真发最优惠实盘，并注明包装、规格、可供数量、最低价格连同最优惠折扣和最早交货期。

3. 如贵方可供所需型号及质量的货物，我们将定期向贵方大量订购。

4. 很高兴附寄我方 345-9 号询盘，请贵方报 FOB 价。

5. 我们想买手工制作的各式真皮鞋，请寄贵方最新商品目录表一份以及详细的价格和支付条件。

6. 请告知贵方能按什么价格、条款及多少数量供应下列商品。

7. 我方拟购 300 辆贵公司经营的"五羊"牌自行车，请电开最优惠 CIF 汉堡价，包括我方的 5%佣金。

8. 请报标的商品的最低价为感。报盘时，请说明包装情况及最早装运期，并寄商品说明书。

9. 我们有一客户对你们的电动机有稳定的需求。请电开 10 台 9 月船期的实盘。

10. 我们想知道订货超过 1000 打能给多少折扣。

V. Letter Writing:

罗宾逊公司（Robinson & Co.）是澳大利亚的一家工艺品进口商，在本行业已有 30 年的经验。他们从其合作伙伴 John & Son Co.得知，宁波钱湖贸易公司是中国主要工艺品出口商。目前该公司对绣花台布感兴趣，希望宁波钱湖公司能寄给他们目录和最新的价格单。请以罗宾逊公司业务员 Kenneth King 的名义写一封询盘信，并以钱湖贸易公司业务员张敏佳的名义给 Kenneth King 回复。

Chapter 4

Offer and Counter-offer

Task 1　Making an Offer

Part I. Introduction

Companies doing business with each other undergo the process of "offer—counter—offer—acceptance" before reaching a sales agreement. This process may be oral, taking the forms of face-to-face meeting or telephone conversations, but mostly it is completed with written correspondence between two companies, e.g., mailed letters and e-mails.

Offers are a formal presentation of the goods to be supplied on the terms specified for the buyer's acceptance. In practice, offers can be divided into two types: firm offers and non-firm offers.

Firm offers are made when sellers promise to sell goods at a stated price within a stated period of time. Non-firm offers are usually indicated by means of sending catalogues, price-lists, proforma invoices and quotations. Contrary to non-firm offers which have no binding force upon the offerer or offeree, firm offers are capable of acceptance and once they have been accepted they cannot be withdrawn.

Part II. Writing Skills

When making a firm offer, the offerer should:

- express thanks for the enquiry
- give favorable comments on the goods needed if possible
- supply all the information requested, including name of commodities, quality, quantity and specifications
- give details of prices, discounts, terms of payment, packing, insurance, date of delivery, etc.
- state clearly the period for which the offer is valid. Usually use such phrases as "subject to your reply reaching us by (before)…", "subject to your reply (acceptance) here within …days" or "this offer is firm (open, valid, good) for …days"
- express hope that the offer will be accepted and assure the customer of good service.

A non-firm offer does not include Point 5, and sometimes might contain even fewer points of the above. In a non-firm offer such phrases are often used as "without engagement (obligation)", "subject to prior sale" or "subject to our final confirmation".

Chapter 4 Offer and Counter-offer

Part III. Sample Letters

Sample 1   A Non-firm Offer

Dear Sirs,

Your letter of January 16th asking us to offer you the embroidered tablecloths has received our immediate attention. We are pleased to be told that there is a ready market for our products in your country.

In compliance with your request, we are making you the following special offer subject to market fluctuations.

Commodity: embroidered tablecloths

Size: 40×70 inches

Price: US$12.00 /pc, CIF Vancouver

Quantity: 3,000 pcs

Price: at US$30 each piece CIF Montreal

Packing: wrapped in see-through plastic bags and packed in standard export cardboard cartons

Payment: by irrevocable L/C, payable by draft at sight

If you find this offer is acceptable, let us have your reply as soon as possible.

                                                                Yours sincerely,

                                                                    (signature)

Notes

1. a ready market   畅销

2. in compliance with your request   应你方要求

3. subject to market fluctuations   以市场波动为准

   subject to   须经……的，有待于……的，以……为条件的，以……为有效

   subject to our final confirmation

   subject to the goods being unsold

   subject to prior sale

4. payable by draft at sight   见票即付

Sample 2   A Firm Offer

Dear Sirs,

We confirm having received your inquiry of August 20 for our gold pens CIF London.

Complying with your request, we are making you a firm offer as follows:

Commodity: Seagull Brand Gold Pens

Specification: as per attached list

Quantity: 1000 dozen

Packing: in cartons of 100 dozen each

Price: at ￡24 per dozen CIFC5 London

Shipment: during October/November, 2007

Payment: by confirmed, irrevocable L/C

This offer is firm, subject to your reply reaching us before September 1.

Please note that we have offered you our most favorable price and thus we are unable to entertain any counter-offer.

We are hoping that you will accept our offer as soon as possible.

Yours faithfully,

(signature)

Notes

1. comply with   按照，遵照

2. confirmed, irrevocable L/C   保兑不可撤销信用证

3. entertain   考虑接受

4. counter-offer   还盘

Task 2   Making a Counter-offer

Part I. Introduction

Sometimes an offeree partly agrees to or totally disagrees with the offer but puts forward his own suggestions. In either case, this is called a counter-offer. In the counter-offer, the buyer may show his disagreement to the certain terms and state his own idea instead. Such alternation, no matter how slight they may appear to be, signify that business has to be negotiated on renewed basis. The original offerer or seller now becomes the offeree and he has full right of acceptance or refusal. He maybe make another counter-offer of his own.

Part II. Writing Skills

When making a counter-offer, the offeree should:

Chapter 4 Offer and Counter-offer

- thank the supplier for the offer
- express regret at inability to accept and state reasons
- put forward amendments or new proposals (an alternative to another offer)
- suggest that there may be other opportunities to do business together

Part III. Sample Letters

Sample 1   Buyer's Counter-offer

Dear Sirs,

　　We acknowledge with thanks receipt of your letter of May 15, 2007 for 300 sets of Butterfly Brand sewing machines at US$60 per set CIF Lagos.

　　In reply, we regret to state that your price has been found too high to be acceptable.

　　As you know, the price of sewing machines has gone down since last year. Some countries are actually lowering their prices. Under such circumstance, it is impossible for us to accept your price, as the goods of similar quality are easily obtainable at a lower figure. If you can make a reduction in your price, say 8%, there is a possibility of getting business done.

　　We expect your early reply.

　　　　　　　　　　　　　　　　　　　　　　　　　　Sincerely yours,

　　　　　　　　　　　　　　　　　　　　　　　　　　　　(signature)

Notes

1. figure   这里指"数字",即"价格"。
2. say 8%   这里是"Let's say 8%"的简化,意思相当于"for example",即"比方说8%"。
3. get business done   意思是"成交",同样意思的表达方法还有: come to business, come to terms, make a bargain, close a deal, conclude business, conclude a transaction 等。

Sample 2   A Letter of Counter-offer for the Purpose of Reducing Prices

Dear Sirs,

　　Thank you for your letter of July 5 offering us your "Sunshine" brand raincoats.

　　To be candid with you, we like your raincoats, but your prices appears to be on the high side as compared with those of makes. It is understood that to accept the prices you quoted would leave us little or no margin of profit on our sales. As you know Kuwait is a developing country, its principal demand is for articles in the medium price range.

　　We appreciate your prompt response to our enquiry and would like to take this opportunity to conclude some transactions with you. We would, therefore, suggest that you make allowance, say 10% on your quoted prices so as to enable us to introduce your products to our customers. If, however, you cannot do so, then we shall have no alternative but to leave the business as it is.

For your information, some parcels from Hong Kong have been sold here at a much lower price. We hope you will consider our counter-offer favorably and let us have your acceptance by telex. It may interest you to know that once you have opened up a market here, you would have every advantage of developing a beneficial trade in the Gulf.

Yours sincerely,
(signature)

Notes

1. make   *n*. 品牌

2. margin of profit   利润

3. price range   价格范围

4. on the high side   （价格）偏高

5. leave the business as it is   使交易维持现状

6. for sb's information   顺告，以供参考

Sample 3 Counter-offer on Delivery

October 14, 2006

Re: Offer No. 328

Dear Smith,

Thank you for your offer dated October 9, 2006. As you know, your toys always sell well in our stores.

While pleased with other terms of your offer, we would hope that due to our long business relationship you could do better with the delivery. It is known that we are trying to put these items on the shelves before the Christmas season. Therefore, we hope to receive them as soon as possible and would ask if you could guarantee delivery within two weeks after receipt of the L/C. We then need time to distribute the goods to each chain store and get the items stocked.

Please let me know if you will be able to accept the delivery schedule.

Chapter 4 Offer and Counter-offer

> I look forward to your immediate answer.
>
> > Sincerely yours,
> >
> > Mary Green
> >
> > Purchasing Manager

Notes

1. guarantee delivery 保证交货
2. distribute *vt./vi.* 分配，分发，散布，分布，分销
3. chain store 连锁商店
4. stock *vt.* 储备，保持……的供应，备货，贮存/*n.* 储备品；（商店的）现货，存货

Sample 4　Declining a Counter-offer

> Dear Sirs,
>
> 　　In reply to your letter of April 6 requesting a 10% reduction in price, we regret we find it very difficult to comply with.
>
> 　　The prices we quoted are closely calculated. Thanks to the excellent quality of our products, considerable business has been done with many customers in European markets at these prices. We believe a fair comparison of quality between our products and similar articles from other sources will convince you of the reasonableness of our quotation. However, in order to help you develop business in this line, we are prepared to allow you a special discount of 3% provided your order calls for a minimum quantity of 8,000 dozen. If you think our proposal acceptable, please let us have your order as soon as possible.
>
> 　　We are anticipating your early reply.
>
> > Yours faithfully,
> >
> > (signature)

Notes

1. decline　*v.* 谢绝，拒绝（语气比 refuse 委婉些）

    e.g. They have to decline orders because of shortage of raw materials.

    　　由于原料缺乏，他们只得谢绝订单。

2. thanks to　多亏，由于

3. We believe a fair comparison of quality between our products and similar articles from other sources will convince you of the reasonableness of our quotation.

我们相信只要把我方产品的质量与其他类似产品相比较，你方就会知道我们的报价是合理的。

  convince sb of sth 使某人相信某事

4. … provided your order calls for a minimum quantity of 8000 dozen.

只要你方能以 8000 打为最低起订量。

Part IV. Useful Expressions and Typical Sentences

Useful Expressions

1. (make an) offer, submit an offering 发盘

2. firm offer 实盘

3. subject to... 以……为准

4. hold an offer open, keep an offer open 留盘

5. withdraw an offer 撤回一项发盘；cancel an offer 撤销一项发盘

6. alter an offer 变更发盘

7. extend an offer 延长发盘有效期

8. comply with one's request 按照某人的要求

9. as requested 按照要求；as stated 如所述；as agreed 如约定

10. specifications 规格

11. offering period 发盘有效期

12. under separate cover / by separate mail 另封，另邮，另寄

13. current price 现价；market price 市价；buying price 买价；selling price 卖价；
  net price 净价；retail price 零售价；wholesale price 批发价

14. net price without commission 不含佣净价

15. offer from stock 供现货；have goods in stock 有现货

16. make delivery 交货

17. without engagement 无约束

18. in view of... 鉴于……，考虑到……

19. quotation sheet 报价单

20. as per attached list 见附页

Chapter 4 Offer and Counter-offer

Typical Sentences

1. It is our usual practice to supply new customers with our goods for payment within one month from date of invoice, in the first instance, and later to extend this term to three months.

2. We cannot consider these prices firm for an indefinite period because of the situation on the coffee market.

3. This offer is firm subject to your immediate reply, which should reach us not later than the end of this month. There is little likelihood of the goods remaining unsold once this particular offer has lapsed.

4. The offer will remain firm until March 31, 2007 beyond which date the terms and prices should be discussed anew.

5. As requested, we are offering you the following, subject to our final confirmation.

6. As our market is now somewhat slow and prices are generally low, you are very fortunate in making purchase at this time.

7. We are pleased to inform you that there are 50 tons of walnuts now available for export.

8. We are pleased to notify you that the whole of our extensive stock of silks, velvets, ribbons, mantles, shawls, woolen and cotton goods, is now on sale at prime cost.

9. Referring to your letter dated July 10 in which you inquired for plastic toys, we have pleasure in cabling you an offer as follows.

10. We are glad to have received your letter dated November 14 for our bicycles. In reply to your inquiry, we are pleased in making you the following offer.

11. We are making you, subject to your acceptance reaching us not later than September 15, 2007, the following offer.

12. We have here cabled you a firm offer until May 31, 2007.

13. We recommend that you take prompt advantage of this offer, which is firm for three days until July 31, 2007.

14. We are making you a firm offer of 30 metric tons walnut meat at Euro € 2500 per metric ton CIF European main ports for November shipment.

15. In reply to your inquiry of yesterday, March 5, 2007, we have pleasure in offering you these at the very low price of HK$11000 per M/T CIF Stockholm, packed in ordinary gunny bags.

16. We regret to inform you that we do not have in stock the goods in the desired quality.

17. Owing to the increased demand for this type of car, our stocks have run very low.

18. As prices are steadily rising we would advise you to place your order without delay.

19. Thank you for your inquiry of September 4 informing us that you find our canned meat satisfactory and that you are considering placing a trial order with us.

20. Further to our letter of December 12, we now offer you, without engagement, our various items as follows.

Part V. Project Training

Project 1

Training Situation:

The letter will be from China Textile Company, 45 Beijing Road, Shanghai, to Clothing Corporation, 1234 Royal Road, Hong Kong. The offer is for the purchase of 400 women's suits and 500 men's suits in blue and black. Women's suits are $500 and men's suits are $400. Discount offered is 2% off the listed price. Prices are FOB Hong Kong. Terms of payment are by L/C. Delivery should be arranged eight weeks after receipt of L/C. Each item is to be packed in a plastic bag with 10 to a carton.

Training Requirements:

Write a letter making an offer according to the above situation.

Project 2

Training Situation:

Mr. Lawrence, General Manager of the United Textiles Company, Ltd. (26 Lawton Street, Liverpool, England), is a large dealer in textiles in England. He is interested in all of the Chinese silk products and now is approaching China National Import & Export Corporation, Shanghai Branch for an offer for specific products.

Hint 1: Interested in silk products and hope to receive the lowest quotation CIF London for 3000 pieces of silk carpets with details of discount and payment terms. Some catalogues and sample cuttings are required.

Hint 2: US$125 per piece CIF London, subject to reply here before May 9. No discount. Payment by an irrevocable L/C available by draft at sight is required. Catalogues and sample cuttings have been airmailed.

Hint 3: Price is higher than those from other suppliers. Suggest a reduction by 10%, otherwise business is impossible.

Chapter 4 Offer and Counter-offer

Training Requirements:

- Write a letter from the exporter to the importer offering 3000 pieces of silk carpets together with some other useful information.
- Make a counter-offer in the name of the importer and point out that the price quoted is too high and ask for a reduction by 10%.

Part VI. Optional Study

I. Related Information

1. Offer and Quotation

An offer is a promise to supply or buy goods on the terms and conditions stated. In an offer, the offerer not only quotes the price of the goods he wishes to sell or to buy but also indicates all necessary terms of transactions for the offeree's consideration and acceptance.

A quotation is not an "offer" in the legal sense. A quotation is merely a notice of the price of certain goods at which the sellers are willing to sell. It is not legally binding as a firm offer if the sellers later decide not to sell. The price is subject to change without previous notice. However, if a quotation is made together with all necessary terms and conditions of sales, it amounts to an offer. So, these two words are sometimes confusing in use.

2. Offer and Bid

An offer is a response made in reply to an inquiry or an expression made voluntarily with a view to expanding business. An offer may be made by a seller or a buyer. A bid refers to the offer made by the buyer. It has the same features as any offers made by the seller.

3. The Significance and Effect of Counter-offer

In international trade, when the offeree accepts the terms and conditions stated in the offer, the transaction is concluded. However, in most cases, the offeree would reject the terms and conditions or state his own terms and conditions by return. The rejection or partial rejection of the offeree to the offer is called counter-offer. A counter-offer is virtually a counter proposal initiated by the original offeree. In a counter-offer, the buyer may show disagreement to the price, or packing, or shipment and state his own terms instead. Once the counter-offer is made, the original offer is no longer valid, and the offeree now becomes the offerer as the counter-offer becomes the new offer.

Counter-offer constitutes the main part of business negotiations. During the negotiation, many issues (such as quality, quantity and packing of the goods, price, shipment, insurance, payment terms, commodity inspection, disputes and settlement of disputes, force majeure, and arbitration, etc.) will be talked about by the sellers and the buyers. So counter-offers are usually time consuming and may go many rounds before business is concluded or dropped.

4. The Contents of an Offer

A satisfactory offer usually includes the following:

- an expression of thanks for the inquiry, if any
- the name of commodities, quality, quantity, packing and specifications
- the details of prices, discounts and terms of payment
- a statement or clear indication of what the prices cover
- the date of delivery
- the period for which the offer is valid

5. Main Contents of a Counter-offer

A satisfactory counter-offer generally includes the following:

- thanking the offerer for his offer and mentioning briefly the contents of the offer
- expressing regret at inability to accept the offer and giving reasons for non-acceptance
- making an appropriate counter-offer
- hoping the counter-offer will be accepted and there may be an opportunity to do business together

II. Supplementary Specimen Letters

Specimen Letter 1

Dear Mr. Crown,

With reference to your enquiry of May 24, we take pleasure in making the following offer:

"5000 pieces of brocade handbags, at US$12.00/pc CIF Vancouver for shipment in August, 2006 for payment by irrevocable documentary L/C in seller's favor, which we hope you will find in order. Please note that this offer is subject to goods being unsold."

As we have received large number of orders from our clients, it is quite probable that our present stock may soon run out. We would therefore suggest that you take advantage of this attractive offer.

Chapter 4 Offer and Counter-offer

> We look forward to receiving your order.
>
> Yours Sincerely,
David Chen

Notes

1. with reference to   关于，就……而言

   e.g. Dear Sir, with reference to your letter of 15 May…

2. We take pleasure in making the following offer.   我们很高兴地向贵公司报盘如下。

3. Please note that   请注意

   e.g. Please note that the market for the goods is rising and our price cannot remain unchanged for long.

4. stock   *n.* 库存，原料

   be out of stock   没有现货，缺货，卖光

   have   即 keep in stock，有货

   goods in stock   现货

   a large stock of   大批存货

   ex stock   即 from stock，在仓库交货，供现货

   e.g. We still have 1000 incense burners in stock.   我们库里还有1000只香炉。

   Please quote us the prices for the silk flowers which can be supplied from stock.
   请给我们报现货供应的绢花的价格。

Specimen Letter 2

Dear Mr. Chen,

  We are in receipt of your letter of June 1 offering 5000 pieces of brocade handbags at US$12.00 /pc, CIF Vancouver.

  In reply, we regret to inform you that our end-users here find your price too high and out of line with prevailing market level here. You may be aware that some Indonesian dealers are lowering their prices. No doubt, there is keen competition in the market.

  We do not deny that the quality of your brocade handbags is slightly better, but the difference in price should, in no case, be as big as 5%. To step up the trade, we, on behalf of our end-users, make counter-offer as follows:

  5000 pieces of brocade handbags, at US$11.40/pc, CIF Vancouver, other terms as per your letter of June 1.

> As the market is declining, we recommend your acceptance.
>
> We are anticipating your early reply.
>
>   Yours sincerely,
>
>   Martin Crown

Notes

1. be in receipt of 即 have received，收到

2. in reply 作为答复

  这个短语可以放在句首，倘若放在一封信的句首，则应写为：

  In reply to your letter of…

  作为答复你方×月×日的来信

  e.g. In reply to your letter dated September 23, we take great pleasure to inform you that the goods under Contract No. 8776 are now ready for shipment.

  兹复贵公司9月23日来信，我们很高兴地告知8776号合同项下之货物即将装运。

3. be out of line with 与……不一致

4. keen competition 激烈的竞争

  还可说：fierce/ intense/ serious/ severe/ tough competition

5. But the difference in price should, in no case, be as big as 5%. 但价差决不会高达5%。

6. As the market is declining… 由于行市下降（行市转疲）……

Part VII. Exercises

I. Translate the following terms and expressions:

A. Into Chinese:

1. subject to   2. with reference to

3. comply with   4. effect shipment

5. offer from stock   6. without engagement

7. at one's earliest convenience   8. extend an offer

9. entertain a counter-offer   10. make a concession to sb.

B. Into English:

1. 报盘   2. 按惯常条例

3. 接受还盘   4. 最优惠价格

5. 在出售中   6. 发盘有效期

Chapter 4　Offer and Counter-offer

7. 促成交易　　　　　　　　　　　8. 实盘

9. 价格偏高　　　　　　　　　　　10. 下述标题项下商品

II. Choose the best answer to complete each of the following sentences:

1. We _____ if you could give us whatever information you can in this respect.
   A. should appreciate　　　　　　B. appreciate
   C. appreciate it　　　　　　　　D. should appreciate it

2. We _____ the fact that the market is declining.
   A. are aware of　　B. aware　　C. aware of　　D. are aware

3. Should your price _____ competitive, we will place a trial order _____ you.
   A. is, with　　B. are, from　　C. is, from　　D. be, with

4. There is steady demand here _____ crocheted curtains of high quality.
   A. in　　B. of　　C. for　　D. on

5. We regret _____ entertain your order for our glass beaded bags as we are in short supply at present.
   A. not able to　　B. are unable to　　C. cannot　　D. our inability to

6. We are pleased to inform you that the item you requested can be supplied _____.
   A. from stock　　B. in stock　　C. out of stock　　D. of stock

7. For all the remaining items the stated dates of delivery are approximate, but _____ would these dates can be exceeded by 20 days.
   A. in no case　　　　　　　　　B. in any case
   C. under any circumstances　　　D. by all means

8. _____ your letter of March 5, we are pleased to inform you that the L/C has been received.
   A. Replying to　　B. Replied to　　C. Replying　　D. Replied

9. We are _____ receipt of your letter of June 15, 2003.
   A. on　　B. from　　C. in　　D. for

10. We recommend _____ a small quantity for trial.
    A. to buy　　B. buy　　C. bought　　D. buying

III. Translate the following sentences into Chinese:

1. With reference to your letter of October 15, inquiring for women's jeans, we enclose our quotation No.213 for your consideration and trust you will find our prices acceptable.

2. Our best offer is given below subject to our final confirmation.

3. We must stress that this offer is good for two days only because of the heavy demand for the limited supplies of these goods in stock.

4. This offer must be withdrawn if not accepted within three days.

5. We wish to state that our quotations are subject to alteration without notice and to our confirmation at the time of placing your order.

6. We are unable to accept your offer as other suppliers have offered us more favorable terms.

7. In order to conclude the transaction, we are prepared to reduce the price to 30 pounds.

8. Considerable quantities have been sold at this price, therefore it is impossible to make any further reduction.

9. If it were not for the friendship between us, we would not have made a firm offer at such a low price.

10. We regret to say that we cannot accept your offer as your price is on the high side.

IV. Translate the following sentences into English:

1. 谢谢贵公司的询盘。我们有大量的男士皮鞋现货供应，很高兴向贵方报盘如下。

2. 此报盘以我方在收到贵公司答复时货物未售出为有效。

3. 这是实盘，以贵方11月6日前电复到此为有效。

4. 如对我方报价感兴趣，请于10月底前用电报接受。

5. 兹确认我方给您的电报发盘，提供20公吨核桃，每吨人民币3500元（CIF欧洲主要口岸价），8月装运。

6. 贵方还盘与现行国际市场不一致。

7. 这确实是我们的底价了。

8. 很遗憾我们无法接受贵方2007年5月10日的还盘。

9. 我们所报的价格是非常具有竞争性的。不过如果你们的订单超过10000件，我们可以提供10%的折扣。

10. 我们最多只能让价5%。

V. Translate the following letter into English:

敬启者：

兹确认收到你方八月四日有关人造棉纱(rayon yarn)的还盘。

我们必须指出我们有关上述商品的报价与其质量完全相符，按此价格我们已收到来自其他客户的大量订单。我们希望提醒你方注意随着季节的临近，行情坚挺且有上涨趋势。

因此，我们很难接受你方的还盘，最多只能各让一半。如有兴趣，望尽早来电接受。

XXX 谨上

VI. Write an English letter based on the following information:

1. 告诉对方你已经收到其 2007 年 9 月 13 日关于中国绿茶（green tea）的还盘信，谢绝对方的还盘。

2. 明确表示很遗憾无法接受对方降价 10%的还盘，并说明按所报价格你们已经收到了大量订单。

3. 强调你们的报价是适中合理的，如果降价 10%你们将无利可图。

4. 建议对方重新考虑你们的报价并表示希望能在双方互利的情况下达成交易。

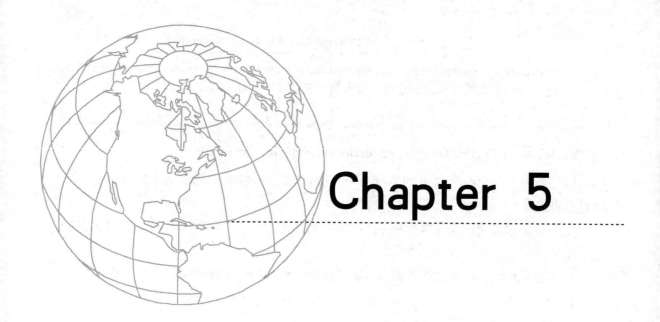

Chapter 5

Conclusion of Business

Chapter 5 Conclusion of Business

Task 1　Placing an Order

Part I. Introduction

An acceptance is a fact that the buyers or sellers agree completely to all the terms and conditions in an offer (or a counter-offer as a new offer). If the offer is a firm offer, a deal is concluded after acceptance. If the offer is a non-firm offer, a deal is not concluded until the acceptance is confirmed by the buyers or sellers.

An order is a request for the supply of a specific quantity of goods. It may result from the buyers' acceptance or confirmation of a firm offer made by the sellers or result from the sellers' acceptance or confirmation of a counter-offer made by the buyers. An order or an order letter should include full details of article number, quantity, specification, quality, unit price, total value, shipment, packing, insurance and terms of payment as agreed upon in preliminary negotiations between the exporter and the importer.

A "first" order or an initial order, an order from a new customer, should be confirmed in the written form. The purpose of doing so is to make sure that both the exporter and the importer have identical understanding of the terms on which they have agreed. Once an order is accepted by the exporter, he must send a letter confirming agreed terms and conditions. Then a transaction is concluded and a contract will be signed between both parties.

Part II. Writing Skills

An order should at least contain the following points:

- description of the goods, such as specification, size, quantity, quality and article number (if any)
- prices (unit prices as well as total prices)
- terms of payment
- mode of packing
- port of shipment, port of destination and time of shipment, etc.

The following structure can be for your reference in placing an order:

- Use direct language in the first paragraph to tell the seller of the buyer's intention to place an order.

- Describe what is being ordered in great detail. Indicate the catalog numbers, sizes, colors, prices, specifications and all other relevant information that will enable the seller to fill the order without any further questions.
- Close the letter by expressing willingness to cooperate or suggesting future business dealings.

Part III. Sample Letters

Sample 1 Buyer's Confirmation of an Order

Dear Sirs,

In reply to your telex of July 19 offering 500 dozen Cotton Blouses at US$110.5 per dozen CIF New York for immediate shipment, we dispatched to you a telex today. For your reference, a copy of the telex is enclosed.

To confirm this order we are enclosing our Purchase Note No.86 including shipping instructions. To ensure prompt execution, we have instructed our banker to open an irrevocable L/C in your favor by cable, which you will receive within a few days.

Please pay your best attention to the shipment.

Faithfully yours,

(signature)

Notes

1. Purchase Note　购货单
2. shipping instructions　装运指示，装运须知
3. by cable　即 by telegram
4. in sb's favor　以某人为受益人

Sample 2 Placing an Initial Order

May 14, 2006

Re: Order No.52765

Dear Wang Lin,

Thank you so much for your letter of April 16 and the catalogs. Pursuant to our e-mail since that date, we have decided to place an initial order as follows:

Item	Item No.	Color	Price($)	Quantity	Subtotal
Blouse	325	Red	10.00	100	1,000.00
		Blue	10.00	100	1,000.00
		Yellow	10.00	100	1,000.00

Chapter 5 Conclusion of Business

		White	10.00	200	1,000.00
Sweater	456	Blue print	15.00	100	1,500.00
Sweater	543	Green print	20.00	200	4,000.00
		Total		800	9,500.00

If this order is executed successfully, we will be placing larger orders in the future.

Please deliver the goods to our warehouse at 643 Front Drive, Newtown, CA 99989. We understand you will be shipping from stock and should expect delivery within one month after you receive our letter of credit. The letter of credit will be prepared as soon as we get your confirmation.

We look forward to a long and successful cooperation.

Sincerely yours,
John Smith
Purchasing Manager

Notes

1. pursuant to 即 according to a particular law, rule, contract，依照，遵循

   e.g. As for our order for 1000 dozen bath towels, pursuant to the outcome of the negotiations between us, we are sending you herewith our P/C in duplicate, one copy of which is to be countersigned and returned immediately for our file.

   关于我方 1000 打浴巾的订单，根据双方磋商结果，随函附上订购确认书一式两份，请速签并退还一份，以便我方存档。

2. initial *adj.* 开始的，最初的

3. print *n.* 印花布

4. warehouse *n.* 仓库

5. ship from stock 发现货

Sample 3 Placing a Repeat Order

Re: Contract No.36PGO22

Tianyan Brand Men's Shirts

Dear Mr. Chen,

We have received the captioned shipment ex. S.S West Wind and are very pleased to

inform you that we find the goods quite satisfactory. As we believe we can sell additional quantities in this market, we wish to place with you a repeat order for 1,800 dozen of the same style and size. If possible, please arrange early shipment of this repeat order, as we are badly in need of the goods.

  In case the said goods are not available from stock, we shall be very grateful to you if you could advise us as to the specifications of those that can be shipped from stock, stating full particulars.

Yours sincerely,

Ronald Gibson

Purchasing manager

Notes:

1. captioned shipment 即 goods mentioned in the subject line，标题所指货物
2. ex S.S. 由……船装运

  per 和 ex 都是介词，在表示由什么货轮装运货物的时候是有区别的，per 主要表示由什么货轮运出，而 ex 表示由什么货轮运入。

3. badly in need of 急需
4. in case 万一，如果

  e.g. In case you are unable to offer us at this time, may we suggest that you quote us an indicative price first?

  如果目前你们不能报价，建议先报给我们一个指示性的价格。

5. particulars *n.* 详情，细目

Task 2 Accepting an Order

Part I. Introduction

  After receiving an order, the seller may immediately confirm the acceptance if he can accept all the terms and conditions stipulated in it. An acceptance or a confirmation is in fact an unreserved assent of the buyers or the sellers.

  As to export business of our country, a trading company may make out a sales confirmation or sales contract (abbreviated as S/C) in duplicate after conclusion of a deal. The company signs the S/C in duplicate and then sends them to the buyer to be countersigned and asks him to send

Chapter 5 Conclusion of Business

back the original to be kept on file. An S/C signed by both parties is binding upon the both. The buyer and the supplier must fulfill their obligation in compliance with it.

Part II. Writing Skills

When accepting an order received, the following structure may be for your reference:

1. Express appreciation for the order received.

2. Assure the buyers that the goods they have ordered will be delivered in compliance with their request. It is also advisable for the sellers to take the opportunity to resell their products or to introduce their other products to the buyers.

3. Close the letter by expressing willingness to cooperate or suggesting future business dealings.

4. Enclose sales contract or sales confirmation in duplicate for counter-signature.

Part III. Sample Letters

Sample 1　Confirming Buyer's Order

Dear Sirs,

　　We are pleased to confirm your order for 500 sets of bicycles amounting to USD 60000.00.

　　As requested, we are preparing to make shipment by the end of this month. We would appreciate it if you could open an irrevocable L/C in our favor as soon as possible, valid until March 15.

　　Upon receipt of your L/C, we will arrange shipment immediately. We hope you will see to it that the L/C stipulations are in exact accordance with those of the sales contract.

　　　　　　　　　　　　　　　　　　　　　　　　　　　　Yours faithfully,

　　　　　　　　　　　　　　　　　　　　　　　　　　　　　　(signature)

Notes

1. amount to　总计，达到，相当于，等于

2. as requested　根据请求，按照请求

3. see to it that　务必……

4. upon receipt of　收到

5. in accordance with　按照或依据某事物

Sample 2 Seller's Acceptance of an Order

Dear Sir or Madam,

　　We have acknowledged your order No.345 and thank you for placing an order with us. We have made arrangements with our manufacturer to assure you that delivery will be punctual.

　　In regard to the terms of payment, we wish to reiterate that our customary practice is by 100% Confirmed, Irrevocable, and Transferable Letter of Credit in our favor to be available by sight draft and to remain valid for negotiation in China until the 15th day after the aforesaid time of shipment. As requested in your previous letter, we have sent you our Sales Confirmation No. 336 in duplicate and look forward to one copy duly countersigned sent by you.

　　We appreciate your faithful cooperation and hope that our handling of this first order of yours will lead to further business between us.

　　We anticipate hearing from you soon.

Yours truly,
(signature)

Notes

1. acknowledge   *v.* 确认收悉，告知收到
2. make arrangements with sb.   与某人安排好
   make arrangements with sth.   安排好某事
3. in regard to   关于，类似的词组有：with regard to, regarding, as regards, as to, as for, concerning, with reference to, referring to
4. reiterate   *v.* 重申
5. customary practice   即 usual practice，习惯做法
6. duly   *adv.* 按时，及时，适当，合适，适度

Task 3 Declining an Order

Part I. Introduction

　　Sometimes, the exporter may find it difficult to accept the importer's order because the goods required are not available or price and specifications have been changed. In this case, letters rejecting orders must be written with the utmost care and with an eye to goodwill and

Chapter 5 Conclusion of Business

future business. It is advisable to recommend suitable substitutes and persuade the importer to accept them.

If turning down an order, the exporter should explain the reason, show appreciation of the importer's confidence in the exporter's company and goods, express regret of inability to be helpful and the wish for future contacts, i.e., be polite and generalize the terms so that the importer does not think this refusal only applies to him.

Part II. Writing Skills

The following organization can be for your reference in writing a letter declining an order:

A Positive Opening: It is sensible to open the letter in a positive way in order to place the message in its correct communication context. For example, appreciation or pleasure in receiving the order can be stated at the beginning of the letter.

Detailed Explanations: When declining an order, detailed and sensible reasons should be provided in order to retain the reader's interest in the writer's products or services. In addition, in order to conclude a deal, the writer usually offers suitable substitutes, makes counter-offers and persuades the buyers to accept them.

A Positive Close: End the letter in the way that makes the reader aware of the writer's expectation for future business relations with him.

Part III. Sample Letters

Sample 1 Seller's Declination of an Order

> Dear Sirs,
>
> Thank you for your order No.233 for black silk which we received today.
>
> We regret that, owing to a shortage of stocks, we are unable to fill your order.
>
> Moreover, our manufacturer cannot undertake to entertain your order for future delivery owing to the uncertain availability of raw materials. We will, however, contact you by E-mail once supply improves.
>
> In the meantime, please feel free to send us your specific enquiries for other types of textiles. You can be assured of our best attention at all times.
>
> Yours faithfully,
>
> (signature)

Notes

    1. fill your order   履行你方订单

    2. raw materials   原料，原材料

    3. in the meantime   在……期间，同时

    4. be assured of   使确信，使放心

    5. at all times   即 at any time，任何时候

Sample 2   Declining to Reinstate Buyer's Order

Dear Sirs,

    We wish to confirm our fax today, a copy of which is enclosed, informing you that we regret our inability to comply with your request to reinstate your Order 113 for Canned Beef, which had been placed by your fax of October 16 and was cancelled later.

    As you are aware, our offer for this commodity was a stock offer, and immediately after your cancellation, all the stock was sold to another company in your market.

    We are very sorry to disappoint you, but hope you will understand that stock offers are a touch-and-go kind of things.

                                                                   Yours truly,

                                                                   (signature)

Notes

    1. comply with   依从，服从，遵从，照做，遵照

    2. reinstate   *vt.* 复原，恢复，复职，恢复原状

    3. cancellation   *n.* 取消，撤销，被取消的事物

    4. touch-and-go   *adj.* 危险的，惊险的，一触即发的，快速行动的

Part IV. Useful Expressions and Typical Sentences

Useful Expressions

    1. to place an order with sb. for sth.   向某人下某货的订单/向某人订购某货

    2. to confirm one's order   确认订单

    3. to be unable to accept /decline one's order   无法接受/拒绝某人订单

    4. We confirm having purchased from you…   兹确认已从你方购妥……

    5. to execute / fulfill an order   执行订单

Chapter 5 Conclusion of Business

6. to sign and return a copy of … for one's file   签退一份……以供某人存档

7. repeat order   续订订单

8. heavy bookings   巨大预订量

9. commit oneself to new orders   承诺新的订单

10. handle one's order with great care   认真履行订单

11. the falling market   市场萧条

12. up to one's expectation   达到某人期望

13. a trial order   试购单

14. have no alternative but to do sth   别无选择只得做……

15. place additional orders   追加订购，额外订购

16. prompt shipment   立即装运

17. an initial order   首次订购

18. come to terms   达成交易

19. a good market for   （商品）畅销

20. on usual terms   按通常条件

Typical Sentences

1. We are pleased to place an order with you for the following items on the understanding that they can be supplied from stock at the prices quoted.

2. Thank you for your quotation of March 5 and the samples of the foot wears, we are pleased to place an order with you on the terms stated in your fax.

3. We are sending you our sales contract No. 5690 in duplicate. Please countersign and return one copy for our file as soon as possible.

4. If the first order is satisfactorily executed, we shall place repeat orders with you.

5. The chief difficulty in accepting your orders now is the heavy backlog of commitments. But you may rest assured that as soon as we are able to accept new orders, we shall give priority or preference to yours.

6. Your order is booked and will be executed with great care. Please open the covering L/C, which must reach here one month before the date of shipment.

7. To avoid any possible dispute, we wish to make it clear that the goods supplied to our Order No.34 must be in exact accordance with the sample in both quality and design.

8. Please follow our shipping instructions carefully and make sure that our order is executed to the entire satisfaction of our customers with the least possible delay.

9. It is regrettable to see an order dropped owing to no agreement on price, however, we wish to recommend you another quality at a lower price for your consideration.

10. While thanking you for your order, we have to say that supplies of raw materials are becoming more and more difficult to obtain, and we have no alternative but to decline your order.

11. We enclose a trial order. If the quality is up to our expectations, we shall send repeat orders in the near future. Your prompt attention to this order will be highly appreciated.

12. We fax you our Order No.112, but must point out that the falling market here will leave us little or no margin of profit. Therefore, your quotation for future orders must be more favorable.

13. If the first order is satisfactorily executed, we shall place repeat orders with you.

14. Thank you for your interest in our stainless cutlery, but we are sorry to inform you that because we have a lot of orders in hand and the factories are heavily committed, we have no more goods available at present.

15. Thank you for your order of May 24 and the samples you sent us. We are pleased to place our order with you as follows.

16. We have booked the following order according to your fax of… and our fax of… and wish to assure you that, upon receipt of the relevant credit, we shall give priority to yours.

17. We highly appreciate your letter of June 4 together with your Order No.692 and are pleased to accept your terms and conditions. Enclosed: please find our Sales Confirmation No. 112 in duplicate, one copy of which should be signed and sent back to complete our records.

18. We are pleased to give you an order for the following items on the understanding that they will be supplied from stock at the prices quoted.

19. With reference to your fax of July 8, we have pleasure in informing you that we have booked your Order No.893 for 1000 dozen blouses. We are sending you our S/C No.100 in duplicate, one copy of which please sign and return for our file.

20. Regarding our requirements for the next quarter, we hope you will see your way to make us an offer. For your reference, we are prepared to take in 20, 000 dozen.

Part V. Project Training

Project 1

Training Situation:

ABC Clothing Corporation is on 1234 Royal Road in Hong Kong. It is going to place a first order from China Textile Company, which is on 45 Beijing Road in Shanghai, for:

Chapter 5　Conclusion of Business

5000 yards of #82 cotton cloth at $11.00 per yard

1000 yards of #75 cotton cloth at $12.00 per yard

1000 yards of #50 cotton cloth at $15.00 per yard

Training Requirements:

Write a letter for the ABC Clothing Corporation. The letter should include terms of payment. You should agree to all other conditions as per the quotation, and inquire when the order will be shipped.

Project 2

Training Situation:

You are a salesman in the Eastern Golden Sun Trading Company. The Western Trading Co. has ordered 30000 pairs of household slippers of your manufacture. You cannot fulfil the order by the date mentioned.

Training Requirements:

The students are required to write a letter from the exporter to the importer for the reason why you cannot fulfill the order by the date mentioned and state clearly when you could deliver.

Part VI. Optional Study

I. Related Information

Repeat Order

Characteristics

A repeat order has nothing special in nature. Anything that appears in an initial order may also be contained in a repeat order. But because of previous experience in dealing with the sellers, the buyers are familiar with the sellers' usual practice as well as the details of their products. As a result, a repeat order may be simpler, with many details omitted.

Points

1. If there is anything that is not satisfactory, the buyer should point it out and ask the seller to make an improvement.

2. To be sure to get exactly what is being ordered, accuracy and clarity are also needed in repeat orders.

Structure

1. Open the letter in a positive way, either expressing satisfaction with the fulfillment of previous orders or directly informing the seller of the buyer's intention to place an order.

2. Describe what is being ordered in detail. If any improvement or change of the business conditions is needed, state it clearly in the letter so as to enable the seller to fill the order promptly and accurately without any further questions.

3. Close the letter with a confident expectation of fulfillment of the order.

Reply to a Repeat Order

1. Appreciation for the repeat order received.

2. Clarification of the specific method of shipment and date of delivery (if the repeat order is accepted) or detailed reasons for having to decline the order and other alternatives to close a deal (if the repeat order has to be declined).

3. The seller's attitude towards the buyer's request for changing or improving business conditions if any. (If the request cannot be met, it's advisable to provide specific reasons and offer other alternatives to conclude a deal.)

4. Expectation for increased opportunities of cooperation.

II. Supplementary Specimen Letter

Specimen Letter 1

Dear Mr. Sutherland,

We were very pleased to receive your letter of May 21 placing a large order with us.

Before we can send the goods, we must ask you for the usual references, one from your bank and one from another firm from whom you have bought goods. We would be glad if you would let us have the names and addresses as soon as possible so that we may write to them. These references will, of course, be treated as private and confidential.

We look forward to hearing from you again soon.

Yours sincerely,

(signature)

Notes

1. reference　证明人，推荐人，证明信，推荐信

2. confidential　机密的

Chapter 5　Conclusion of Business

Specimen Letter 2

HUAXIN TRADING CO., LTD.
14TH FLOOR KINGSTAR MANSION
676 JINLIN RD., SHANGHAI, CHINA

Dear Sir or Madam,

　　We are pleased to confirm the cables exchanged between us. From your yesterday's cable we found the quality is up to the standard and the price you quote is satisfactory. In order to promote our business relations and our friendship, we accept your 6% discount, we therefore airmail you our Order No.132 as follows:

Commodity	Quantity	Article	Unit Price	Total
Ladies' sweaters	400 pieces	1123	$20.00	$8,000.00
Children's sweaters	200 pieces	1124	$15.00	$3,000.00
				$11,000.00

　　The L/C will be opened by Bank of China in 15 days in favor of your company. Please note that the sales season is drawing near and the goods are urgently required in our market. We appreciate it if you can dispatch the goods as soon as possible.

Yours faithfully,
(signature)

Notes

1. up to the standard　达到标准，符合标准
2. in favor of　以……为受益人
3. draw near　靠近，临近，即将来临

Specimen Letter 3

Dear Sirs,

　　We have the pleasure of acknowledging your letter of October 6th, in which you inform us that you are satisfied with our men's shirts shipped to you per s.s. "Dongfeng". We also note that you wish to book a repeat order.

　　Much to our regret, we cannot at present entertain any fresh orders for Tiantan Brand Men's Shirts, owing to heavy commitments.

　　However, we are keeping your enquiry before us and as soon as we are in a position to

accept new orders, we will contact you telegraphically.

　　Regarding stock shirts, we are enclosing a list for your perusal. If you are interested in any of our stock goods, please let us know your detailed requirements, stating quantity, size, style, etc.

Yours truly,

David

Sales Manager

Encl.

Notes

1. acknowledge　*v.* 告知（收到），承认

　　e.g. We acknowledge your letter of March 5.　即 We acknowledge (the) receipt of your letter of March 5.

2. per　*prep.* 每，由，由……装运

　　e.g. This material sells at US$×× per metric ton CIF.

　　　　We advise having shipped Contract No.425 per s.s. Peace.

3. keep your enquiry before us　记住你方的询盘

　　也可以说 keep your enquiry in mind 或 keep your enquiry on file for future reference。

4. for your perusal　供你方详阅

Part VII. Exercises

I. Translate the following terms and expressions:

A. Into Chinese:

1. initial order　　　　　　　　　2. suspend an order

3. the captioned shipment　　　　 4. in triplicate

5. book one's order　　　　　　　 6. from stock

7. for our file　　　　　　　　　　8. turn down an order

9. expand our business　　　　　　10. sales confirmation

B. Into English:

1. 达成交易　　　　　　　　　　　2. 取消订单

3. 大量存货　　　　　　　　　　　4. 可供现货

5. 急需　　　　　　　　　　　　　6. 会签

Chapter 5　Conclusion of Business

7. 随后的修改　　　　　　8. 替代产品

9. 供某人详阅　　　　　　10. 弥合差距

II. Choose the best answer to complete each of the following sentences:

1. We were satisfied with the products _____ S.S. Wanjie when your shipment reached us.

　A. per　　　　　B. onto　　　　　C. ex　　　　　D nearby

2. We would be _____ if you would send the goods as soon as possible.

　A. appreciate you　　B. grateful　　　C. thank you　　D pleasing

3. As the captioned shipment is satisfactory to us, we wish to _____ with you. Which of the following expressions is false?

　A. place orders　　　　　　　　　B. book further orders

　C. have repeats　　　　　　　　　D. place repeat orders

4. We are pleased to confirm _____ with you a transaction of 10000 sets of computer monitors.

　A. to have closed　　　　　　　　B. having concluded

　C. concluding　　　　　　　　　D. closing

5. We will expedite _____ of the order.

　A. carrying out　　B. perform　　　C. fulfill　　　D. execution

6. The shipment is of special _____ to us, for products are selling fast in the market.

　A. interests　　　B. interested　　C. interesting　　D. interest

7. Please supply the following items _____ the understanding that the commission is 5% on each in order No.256.

　A. on the basis of　B. based on　　　C. on　　　　D. on the terms of

8. We hope to book _____ you a repeat order _____ the following lines _____USD230 per set CIF London.

　A. from, for, at　　B. for, of, on　　C. with, for, at　　D. \, with, on

9. We are sorry we cannot give you an immediate answer. We have to _____ your request to our head office.

　A. admit　　　　B. summit　　　　C. permit　　　D. submit

10. We are _____ the contract and will send it to you for signature once it is ready.

　A. drawing　　　B. drawing on　　C. drawing up　　D. drawing upon

III. Fill in the blanks with correct forms of the words given below:

A. satisfy

1 The quality of your new product _____ us in every respect.

2. We assure you that the goods will turn out to the _____ of your end-users.

3. We are not quite _____ with the shipment.

4. We are confident that this order will be _____ to you.

B. regard

1. In _____ to S/C No.1360, please ship the goods without delay.

2. As _____ the balance, we'll advise you the position in a few days.

3. We _____ this as a good beginning.

4. We know nothing _____ the market condition there.

C. regret

1. We find it _____ that you failed to book the shipping space on S.S. "Asia".

2. We expressed _____ at the delay.

3. We are _____ that we can not supply the entire quantity required.

4. It is _____ that the matter should still be hanging unsettled.

IV. Fill in the appropriate words or expressions listed below:

1. for your good cooperation   2. in duplicate   3. duly countersigned   4. prove satisfactory

5. for your file   6. in the meantime   7. repeat order   8. enclosing   9. in your favor

Dears Sirs,
  Thank you for your letter of March 2 _____ S/C No. 321 _____ one copy of which we have _____ and are returning one copy _____. _____, we have established the necessary L/C _____. If the first shipment of 80 tons should_____, we would most likely send you _____ for another 50 tons.
  We thank you again _____.

                    Yours faithfully,

                      (signature)

V. Fill in the blanks with suitable prepositions:

1. We appreciate your effort _____ pushing the sale of our products these years.

2. The L/C established _____ our favour does not conform _____ the terms stated in our S/C.

3. Enclosed: please find the duplicate _____ our counter-signature.

4. Your offer is not interesting _____ us.

5. We wish to invite your attention _____ the fact that the shipped goods are badly damaged _____ their arrival.

Chapter 5 Conclusion of Business

6. The L/C, we believe, will reach you _____ due course.

7. We have pleasure _____ sending you sales confirmation No.786 _____ duplicate _____ 3,000 metric tons _____ soybean, one copy _____ which please sign and return to us _____ our file.

VI. Translate the following sentences into English:

1. 这些是仅有的存货。
2. 因制造厂接到太多订货，我们只能答应三月份装船。
3. 如果你没有"蝴蝶"牌缝纫机的现货，请告知其他牌子可供现货的规格及详细情况。
4. 我们高兴地确认从你处购进了300吨钢板。
5. 请放心，一旦新货源到来，我们立刻与您联系。
6. 我们同意按以下条款售出下列商品。
7. 关于下季度我们需要的货物，希望你公司能设法给以报盘。为供参考我们愿订20000打。
8. 很高兴地告知你们：已按你们传真中列明的条款接受你们的订货了。
9. 如无208型现货，请取消此订单。我们对任何代用品都不感兴趣。
10. 质量必须与样货相符。

VII. Translate the following letter into English:

敬启者：

我们感谢你方第AB181号订单，订购200台SP2002型电视摄像机。

我们很愿意向你方提供此货，但目前不能执行该订单，因为有些部件没有货。然而我方可提供品质非常类似的SP2001型货号，可供现货。该型号品质仅次于SP2002型，但价格低8%，可能更适合你方市场。

我们希望该建议能为你方接受。可以肯定，我们会非常认真履行你方订单，使你方完全满意。

VIII. Write a letter ordering the items listed below, specifying quantity, unit price, total amount and terms of payment, shipment:

品名	数量	货号	价格	价格条件
不粘锅	3500	26"	USD121 per set	CFRD3 Chicago
	1400	30"	USD164 per set	CFRD3 Chicago
付款方式	即期汇票信用证			
装运时间	12月25日之前及时抵达			

Chapter 6

Terms of Payment

Chapter 6 Terms of Payment

Task 1   Negotiating Payment Terms

Part I. Introduction

Payment plays an important role in foreign trade. It is often complicated. The mode of payment for each transaction is to be agreed upon between the two trading parties at the time of placing an order. The most frequently adopted mode of payment in foreign trade is letter of credit. The final result of all business activities should be to recover the value of goods supplied or services rendered. If payment is not ensured, then all will be meaningless. So it is vitally important to ensure payment in a sound way.

The most generally used modes of payment in the international trade are: Remittance (M/T, T/T, D/D), Collection (D/A, D/P) and Letter of Credit (L/C).

1. Remittance

Remittance means the payer (usually the buyer) remits a certain sum of money in accordance with the parties' agreement to the payee (usually the seller) through a bank. Payer may remit the sum in the following manner:

(1) Mail Transfer(M/T)

(2) Telegraphic Transfer(T/T)

(3) Demand Draft(D/D)

This method of payment is often used for down payment, payment of commission and for sample, settlement of claim, or as performance bond, etc.

2. Collection

Collection means that the creditor (the exporter) entrusts the bank to collect payment from the debtor (importer). The bank acts as the intermediary.

Parties to a Collection:

(1) drawer or principal

(2) drawee

(3) remitting bank

(4) collecting bank

Types of Collection:

(1) clean collection

(2) documentary collection

There are two types of documentary collection: documents against payment, documents against acceptance. According to the different time of payment, it is divided into D/P at sight and D/P after sight.

Sometimes when the financial standing of an importer is sound or where a previous course of business has inspired the exporter with confidence that the importer will be good for payment, the exporter may accept payment by collection(D/P, D/A)through a bank.

3. Letter of Credit

Letter of credit (L/C) is the most widely used mode of payment, because it is reliable by the exporter who performs in strict accordance with the L/C stipulations. Payment by L/C facilitates trade with unknown buyers and protects both exporters and importers.

As far as the seller's benefit is concerned, L/C is better than D/P, and D/P at sight is better than D/P after sight, whereas D/P is better than D/A. Remittance is only used in small deals.

Letters regarding payment often fall into the following types: discussing mode of payment, urging establishment of L/C, amending L/C or asking for extension of L/C.

Part II. Writing Skills

For letters negotiating payment terms:

Step 1: Show thanks for the letter received.

Step 2: Show regret being unable to accept the other party's opinion.

Step 3: Give enough reasons.

Step 4: Show writer's suggestion.

Step 5: Show expectation.

Part III. Sample Letters

Sample 1 Asking for Payment by T/T

Dear Sirs,

    We thank you for your Letter of August 8 offering us 3000 dozen Bed Covers, but regret very much being unable to accept your terms of payment.

    Payment by L/C is rather inconvenient to a customer like us who often places medium-sized orders. After long years of satisfactory trading, we feel that we are entitled to easier terms. Most of our suppliers are in fact supplying us on T/T or D/P basis.

Chapter 6 Terms of Payment

> Considering the small amount involved in this transaction, we shall be grateful if you will allow us to pay 30% of the total value for this order by T/T and the balance by D/P.
>
> Your accommodation in this respect will be conducive to further development of our business.
>
> Please take the above into careful consideration and fax us your confirmation early.
>
> Yours faithfully,
(signature)

Notes

1. terms of payment   付款方式

   常见的付款方式有：

   (1) L/C (Letter of Credit)   信用证付款

       Documentary L/C   跟单信用证

       Irrevocable L/C   不可撤销信用证

       L/C at sight   即期付款信用证

   (2) Remittance   汇付

       T/T (Telegraphic Transfer)   电汇

       M/T (Mail Transfer)   信汇

       D/D (Demand Draft)   票汇

   (3) Collection   托收

       D/P (Document against Payment)   付款交单

       D/A (Document against Acceptance)   承兑交单

2. be inconvenient to   对……不方便

3. place medium-sized orders   适量订购

   medium-sized   中等大小的

   place a large order with sb   向某人大量订购

   place a trial order with sb   向某人试订购

4. be entitled to   有资格

5. total value   总价值

6. balance   余额

   e.g. They want to have 80% of the goods for the first shipment and the balance for the second.

   我们第一批想要运出货物的80%，其余部分第二批运出。

For the balance of 30 M/Ts under this contract, we would like you to establish a letter of credit before the end of November. 关于本合同的其余 30 公吨货物，我们希望你方在 11 月底前开立信用证。

7. accommodate   适应，和解，通融

   e.g. We will try our utmost to accommodate you.   我们将尽力给予照顾。

   We regret we cannot accommodate you in this respect.   非常抱歉在这一方面我们不能给予通融。

8. be conducive to   *vt.* 有助于（增进，导致）．

Sample 2   Requesting Payment by D/A

Dear Sirs,

Re: Your new style baby wear

　　Thank you for your letter of May 8 concerning your new style baby wear. We are interested in your product and wish to discuss further about it.

　　We noticed that you require payment by letter of credit. However we would like to propose payment by D/A for this first order, as this is a new product and we are not able to make purchase on our own account. We hope to place substantial orders once the demand for this product has been ascertained.

　　We believe our proposal is a reasonable way to test the market and hope you will be willing to cooperate with us.

Yours faithfully,

(signature)

Notes

1. propose   提议，建议

2. on one's own account   为自己（自行负责，依靠自己）

3. place substantial orders   大量订购

   place large orders   大量订购

4. ascertain   *vt.* 确定，查明

5. cooperate with   协作（与……合作，配合）

   e.g. If they can cooperate with each other, everything should run smoothly.
   如果他们能互相配合，一切都会顺利的。

Chapter 6 Terms of Payment

Sample 3 Declining Payment by D/A

Dear Sirs,

   Subject: Your Proposal for Making Payment by D/A

   We are glad to learn from your letter of May 15 that you are interested in our new style baby wear. We also notice that you wish to make payment by D/A.

   We have considered your proposal but regret to say that we cannot accept it, as we do not have sufficient credit information to offer you D/A terms at present.

   However in order to help you push the sales of our new product, we are prepared to accept payment by D/P at sight.

   This is the best thing we can do. Please supply two bank references.

   We have already concluded business with several buyers from Europe and North America. We are pleased to inform you that our new style baby wear is getting popular on the market. We have even received some repeat orders. We hope this will encourage you to place an order with us.

   We are looking forward to receiving your order soon.

Yours faithfully

(signature)

Notes

1. sufficient *adj.* 充足的
2. push the sales 促销
3. accept payment by D/P at sight 接受即期付款交单
4. conclude business 达成交易
5. inform sb that 通知某人某事，that 后接从句

    inform sb of sth 通知某人某事，of 后接名词或动名词
6. repeat order 续订单
7. place an order with sb 向某人订购

Sample 4 Accepting Payment by D/P

Dear Sir or Madam,

   We confirm having received your trial order of January 25 for 1000 pieces folding bicycles.

   While we appreciate your order and your intention of introducing our products into your

market, we have to point out that we generally do business with new customer on sight L/C basis. However, in view of our future business, we are prepared to accept exceptionally payment by sight D/P this time. A sight draft will be drawn on you through our bank to collect the value of the goods as soon as they are shipped.

 It is necessary for us to make it clear that our concession in payment is only for this transaction, which should in no case be taken as a precedent.

Yours faithfully,
(signature)

Notes

1. trial order   试订单

2. point out   指出

3. do business with sb   与某人做业务

4. on sight L/C basis   基于即期付款信用证

5. in view of   鉴于，同 considering

6. sight D/P (sight document against payment)   即期付款交单

7. draw on sb   向某人开立汇票

8. collect   *vt.* 收取（款、税等），托收

  e.g. The company could save money by improving the way it collects accounts.
   如果改变收款方式，这家公司就能节约一些费用。
   As soon as the goods are ready, please fax us and we'll send a container truck to collect.
   一俟货物备妥，请传真我方，我们将派集装箱卡车去收货。

 collection   *n.* 收款，托收

  e.g. The draft together with a full set of documents is to be sent to the Bank of China, Beijing for documentary collection.
   汇票连同全套单据一起交到北京中国银行进行跟单托收。

9. make it clear that   使明确，说明

10. concession   退让，让步

11. transaction   *n.* 交易   conclude transaction 成交

12. take as a precedent   作为先例

 precedent   *n.* 先例

  e.g. It must be clearly understood that, in doing so, we are not setting/establishing a precedent.
   必须说明的是，这次我们这样做，但下不为例。

Chapter 6 Terms of Payment

Task 2 Urging & Advising Establishment of an L/C

Part I. Introduction

The procedures for issuing an L/C are as follows:

1. The buyer and the seller conclude a sales contract providing payment by documentary credit.

2. The buyer instructs his bank—the "issuing" bank to issue a credit in favor of the seller (beneficiary).

3. The issuing bank asks another bank—the advising bank, usually in the country of the seller, to advise and perhaps also to add its confirmation to the documentary credits.

4. The advising or confirming bank informs the seller that the credit has been issued.

Part II. Writing skills

For letters urging establishment of an L/C:

Step 1: To mention the relative contract (order, sales confirmation/contract) number.

Step 2: To stress not having received the covering L/C.

Step 3: To urge the buyer to arrange L/C establishment and related matters.

Step 4: To express the seller's requirements and expectation.

Part III. Sample Letters

Sample 1 Urging Establishment of an L/C

Dear Sir or Madam,

With reference to your order No.123 for 2000 sets Haier Brand Air Conditioner under S/C 168, we'd like to invite your attention to the fact that we haven't received your L/C until now.

Please do your utmost to rush the L/C establishment so that we can execute the contract smoothly.

In order to avoid subsequent amendments, please see to it that the L/C stipulations are in exact conformity with the terms and conditions of the S/C 168.

We hope to receive your good news soon.

Yours sincerely,

Clark

Notes

1. with reference to   兹谈及……常用于商业书信的开始，表示事由，类似的表达法还有：We refer to…, Referring to…, make reference to 或 Reference is made to…。

   e.g. Referring to your letter of March 3 ordering 500 M/T Groundnut Kernels.

   兹谈及你方3月3日订购500公吨花生仁的来函。

2. S/C   sales contract 或 sales confirmation 的缩写

3. invite one's attention   吸引某人的注意力，同意词组有：call one's attention, draw one's attention

4. do one's utmost   尽力

5. rush the L/C establishment   催开信用证，同意词组：urge the establishment of L/C

6. execute the contract   履行合同，执行合同

7. see to it that   确保

8. stipulation   条款，规定

9. in exact conformity with   与……完全一致

10. terms and condition   条款

Sample 2A Urging Establishment of an L/C

April 8, 2000

J.B Lawson & Company

854 San Francisco, California

Dear Sir or Madam,

   We refer to your order NO.789 for 1000 dozen pairs of Viva Jeans.

   We would like to remind you that the delivery date is approaching and we have not yet received the covering letter of credit.

   We would be grateful if you could expedite establishment of the L/C so that we can ship the order in time.

   In order to avoid any further delay, please make sure that L/C instructions are in precise accordance with the terms of the contract.

   We look forward to receiving your reply at an early date.

Yours Sincerely,

China National Textiles Imp.& Exp. Corp.

Chapter 6 Terms of Payment

Notes

1. urge   *vt.* 催促，劝说

   e.g. Recently they have been urging us for execution of their order for 3000 gross pencils.

2. establishment   *n.* 开立，建立

   e.g. We are arranging for the establishment of the relative L/C with the bank at this end.
   我们正安排此地银行开立有关信用证。

   We take this opportunity to approach you for the establishment of trade relations with you.
   我们借此机会与你们联系，希望与你们建立贸易关系。

   establish   *vt.* 开立，开设，确立，建立

   establish an L/C   开立信用证

   open an L/C   即 issue an L/C，开立信用证

   e.g. We hope to establish mutually beneficial business relations with all prospective customers.
   我们希望与所有潜在的客户建立互利的贸易关系。

3. covering L/C   相关信用证

   covering 意为相关的，同 relative L/C

4. We would be grateful if you…   如果你们……，我们将万分感激。

5. expedite establishment of the L/C   加快开立信用证

   rush establishment of the L/C   催开信用证

   in precise accordance with   与……严格一致

4. terms of the contract   合同条款

Sample 2B   Reply to Urging Establishment of an L/C

Dear Sir or Madam,

We would like to draw your attention to our order No.789 for 1000 dozen pairs of Viva Jeans.

On 9 April, an irrevocable, confirmed L/C, which expires on 15 June, has been opened in your favor for an amount of US$250 000 with Chase Manhattan Bank, Inc. in San Francisco. We shall appreciate it if you will expedite the shipment of our order as soon as possible, thus enabling them to catch the brisk demand at the start of the season. We must stress that any delay in shipping the order will involve us in problems with our buyers which could affect our future business.

外贸英语函电

> Thank you in advance for your cooperation.
>
> Yours truly,
J. B. Lawson & Company

Notes

1. draw one's attention to   吸引某人注意力，类似的短语有：call one's attention to, invite one's attention to.

2. an irrevocable/confirmed L/C   不可撤销的、保兑的信用证

3. in one's favor   以某人为受益人

4. expedite the shipment   加速装运

   expedite   *vt.* 加速

   e.g. We will appreciate it if you expedite your offer.

   如能尽快报盘，将不胜感激。

5. brisk demand   需求量大

   brisk   *adj.* 活跃的、兴旺的

   e.g. The market is brisk.   市场繁荣。

   Fashion goods are in brisk demand in our market.   我处市场对时尚商品有大量需求。

6. cooperation   *n.* 合作

Sample 3   Advising Establishment of an L/C

> **INDUSTRIAL AND COMMERCIAL BANK OF CHINA**
>
> ADVICE OF LETTER OF CREDIT   HUAIAN BRANCH
>
> 信用证通知书
>   81 WEST HUAIAN ROAD HUAIAN CHINA
>   TEL: (0086)517-83916666
>   FAX: (0086)517-83999100
>   SWIFT BIC: ICBKCNBJHYC
>   E-MAIL: INTL-HA@JS.ICBC.COM.CN
>
> **TO**（致）：   **DATE**（日期）：16.APRIL 2009
> 淮安市利润对外贸易有限公司
>
> **OUR REF NO.**（我行通知编号）：AV061050900131   (PLEASE ALWAYS QUOTE)
> **L/C NO.**（信用证号）：DC TAO910536
> **DATE OF ISSUE**（开证日）：15.APRIL 2009
> **ISSUER**（开证方）：HONGKONG AND SHANGHAI BANKING CORPORATION

LIMITED, CHINA

    L/C AMOUNT（信用证金额）：USD 37,666.08

    EXPIRE DATE（有效期）：15.JULY 2009

    LATEST SHIPMENT DATE（最迟装运期）：5.JULY 2009

DEAR SIRS（敬启者），

WE HAVE PLEASURE IN ADVISING YOU, THAT WE HAVE RECEIVED FROM THE A/M BANK A LETTER OF CREDIT, CONTENTS OF WHICH ARE AS PER ATTACHED SHEET(S). THIS ADVICE AND THE ATTACHED SHEET(S) MUST ACCOMPANY THE RELATIVE DOCUMENTS WHEN PRESENTED FOR NEOGIATION.

兹通知贵司，我行收到上述银行信用证一份，现随附通知，贵司交单时，请将本通知书及信用证一并提示。

PLEASE NOTE THAT THIS ADVICE DOES NOT CONSTITUTE OUR CONFIRMATION OF ABOVE L/C NOR DOES IT CONVEY ANY ENGAGEMENT OR OBLIGATION ON OUR PART.

本通知书不构成我行对此信用证之保兑及其他任何责任。

IF YOU FIND ANY TERMS AND CONDITIONS IN THE L/C WHICH YOU ARE UNABLE TO COMPLY WITH AND / OR ANY ERROR(S), IT IS SUGGESTED THAT YOU CONTACT APPLICANT DIRECTLY FOR NECESSARY AMENDMENT(S) SO AS TO AVOID ANY DIFFICULTIES WNICH MAY ARISE WHEN DOCUMENTS ARE PRESENTED.

如本信用证中有无法办到的条款及/或错误，请直接与开证申请人联系进行必要的修改，以排除交单时可能发生的问题。

适用规则：SUBJECT TO LATEST VERSION

IF YOU HAVE ANY FURTHER QUERIES, PLEASE DON'T HESITATE TO CONTACT US ON THE ABOVE MENTIONED NUMBER.

如果贵司有任何疑问，请按上述业务编号与我行联系。

THIS IS A COMPUTER-GENERATED LETTER, NO SIGNATURE REQUIRED.

Own BIC/TID   :II: ICBKCNBJJSP BIC identified as:

                                    INDUSTRIAL AND COMMERCIAL BANK

                                    OF CHINA, JIANGSU PROVINCIAL BRANCH

	404, ZHONGSHAN ROAD EAST
	210002 NANJING, China
SWIFT Message Type	:MT:700 Issue of Documentary Credit
Correspondents BIC/TID	:IO: HSBCTWTPOBU BIC resolved to different department HSBCTWTPCBS HONGKONG AND SHANGHAI BANKING CORPORATION LIMITED, China
Sequence of Total	:27:1/1
Form of Documentary Credit	:40A:IRREVOCABLE
Documentary Credit Number	:20:DC TAO910536
Date of Issue	:31C:2009.04.15
Applicable Rules	:40E:UCP LATEST VERSIO
Date and Place of Expiry	:31D:2009.07.15 CHINA
Applicant	:50:LONGFIELD LTD
	C/O NO.1, 9F-4,
	FU HSING NORTH ROAD,
	TAIPEI, CHINA
Beneficiary	:59:HUAIAN LIRUN FOREIGN TRADE CO., LTD. HUAIAN 23 EAST BEIJING ROAD, HUAIYIN DISTRICT HUAIAN CITY JIANGSU 223300, CHINA
Currency Code, Amount	:32B:USD 37,666.08
Maximum Credit Amount	:39B:NOT EXCEEDING
Available with …By…	:41D:ANY BANK IN CHINA BY PAYMENT
Draft at …	:42C:SIGHT FOR FULL INVOICE VALUE
Drawee	:42D:ISSUING BANK
Partial Shipments	:43P:NOT ALLOWED
Transshipment	:43T:ALLOW
Port of Loading/Airport of Departure	:44E:SHANGHAI, CHINA
Port of Discharge/Airport of Destination	:44F:ANIOWERP

Latest Date of Shipment :44C:2009.07.05

Description of Goods and/or :45A: Services

FOB SHANGHAI, CHINA

CHRISTMAS DECORATION

24,216 PCS, DETAIL PER PO S9CCE06901

Documents Required :46A:

+INVOICE IN ONE ORIGINAL AND ONE COPY.

+PACKING LIST IN ONE ORIGINAL AND ONE COPY.

+FULL SET OF ORIGINAL CLEAN 'ON BOARD' BILLS OF LANDING, SHOWING SHIPPER AS: LONGFIELD LTD., SHOWING CONSIGNEE AS: COD'EVENTS 7, RUE AMPERE 67118 GEISPOLSHEIM-GARE STRASBOURG FRANCE, MARKED 'FREIGHT COLLECT', SHOWING NOTIFY PARTY:

1. SAME AS CONSIGNEE

2. SEDIS LOGISTICS BELGIUM SA/NV ZI DE TOURNAI-OUEST II RUE DES SABLIERES 7 B-7522 BLANDAIN BELGIUM

TEL：+32(0)69.33.27.27   FAX：+32(0)69.33.28.28

+FAX COPY OF INSPECTION CERTIFICATE ISSUED APPLICANT CERTIFYING THAT GOODS ARE INSPECTED OK BEFORE SHIPMENT.

+CERTIFICATES OF ORIGIN IN ONE ORIGINAL, SHOWING IMPORTER AS:

COD'EVENTS 7, RUE AMPERE 67118 GEISPOLSHEIM-GARE STRASBOURG FRANCE.

+HEALTHY CERTIFICATE IN ONE ORIGINAL, SHOWING IMPORTER AS:

COD'EVENTS 7, RUE AMPERE 67118 GEISPOLSHEIM-GARE STRASBOURG FRANCE.

Additional Conditions : 47A:

+INSURANCE TO BE COVERED BY ULTIMATE BUYER.

+THIRD PARTY DOCUMENTS ARE ACCEPTABLE.

+UNLESS OTHERWISE EXPRESSLY STATED, DOCUMENTS OTHER THAN DRAFT(S), INVOICE(S) MUST NOT SHOW THE UNIT PRICE, VALUE OF GOODS OR THIS DC NUMBER.

+UNLESS OTHERWISE EXPRESSLY STATED, ALL DOCUMENTS SHOULD BEAR THEIR RESPECTIVE ISSUING DATES.

+UNLESS OTHERWISE EXPRESSLY STATED, ALL DOCUMENTS CALLED FOR UNDER THE CREDIT MUST BE IN YHE LANGUAGE OF THE CREDIT.

+IN ACCORDANCE WITH PROVISIONS OF ARTICLE 16 C (III) (B) OF UCP600, IF WE GIVE NOTICE OF REFUSAL OF DOCUMENTS PRESENTED UNDER THIS CREDIT WE SHALL HOWEVER RETAIN THE RIGHT TO ACCEPT A WAIVER OF DISCREPANCIES FROM THE APPLICANT AND, SUBJECT TO SUCH WAIVER BEING ACCEPTABLE TO US, TO RELEASE DOCUMENTS AGAINST THAT WAIVER WITHOUT REFERENCE TO THE PRESENTER PROVIDED THAT NO WRITTEN INSTRUCTIONS TO THE CONTRARY HAVE BEEN RECEIVED BY US FROM THE PRESENTER BEFORE THE RELEASE OF THE DOCUMENTS. ANY SUCH RELEASE PRIOR TO RECEIPT OF CONTRARY INSTRUCTIONS SHALL NOT CONSTITUTE A FALLURE ON OUR PART TO HOLD THE DOCUMENTS AT THE PRESENTER'S RISK AND DISPOSAL, AND WE WILL HAVE NO LIABILITY TO THE PRESENTER IN RESPECT OF ANY SUCH RELEASE.

+A USD100.00 FEE SHOULD BE DEDUCTED FROM THE REIMBURSEMENT CLAIM FOR EACH PRESENTATION OF DISCREPANT DOCUMENTS UNDER THIS DOCUMENTERY CREDIT. NOT WITHSTANDING ANY INSTRUCTIONS TO THE CONTRARY, THIS CHARGE SHALL BE FOR THE ACCOUNT OF THE BENEFICIARY.

+ONCE DC EXPIRED AND/OR OVER DRAWN INCURRED AND ACCEPTED BY APPLICANT AND DC ISSUING BANK, DC EXPIRED/OVER DRAWN COMMISSION CALCULATED AT 0.25 PCT PER QUARTER (MINIMUM USD 40.00) IS FOR THE ACCOUNT OF BENEFICIARY AND WILL BE DEDUCTED FROM PROCEEDS AT TIME OF REIMBURSEMENT.

+REIMBURSEMENT/PAYMENT FEE OF USD100.00 AND RELATED CABLE FEE FOR EACH PRESENTATION IS FOR ACCOUNT OF BENEFICIARY AND IT WILL BE DEDUCTED FROM THE PROCEEDS AT PAYMENT.

+PRESENTATION OF MULTIPLE SETS OF DOCUMENTS IS NOT ALLOWED. AN ADDITIONAL FEE OF USD100.00 OR EQUIVALENT FOR EACH ADDITIONAL SET OF DOCUMENT WILL BE DEDUCTED FROM THE PROCEEDS.

+UNLESS OTHERWISE STIPULATED, ALL CHARGES EXCEPT DC OPENING CHARGE ARE FOR ACCOUNT OF BENEFICIARY.

+DOCUMENTS MUST BE DESPATCHED IN ONE LOT BY COURIER TO THE ISSUING BANK: THE HONGKONG AND SHANGHAI BANKING CORPORATION

Chapter 6 Terms of Payment

LIMITED, 16F, BUILDING G, NANKANG SOFTWARE PAPK, NO.3-1, YUAN QU STREET, NANKANG DISTRICT, TAIPEI 115 CHINA ATTN: TRADE AND SUPPLY CHAIN.

Period for Presentation	:48:WITHIN 10 DAYS AFTER THE DATE OF SHIPMENT BUT WITHIN THE VALIDITY OF THE CERDIT.
Confirmation Instructions	:49:WITHOUT
Inst/Paying/Accept/Negotiate Bank	:78:

+ON RECEIPT OF DOCUMENTS CONFORMING TO THE TERMS OF THIS DOCUMENTARY CREDIT BY THE ISSUING BANK, WE UNDERTAKE TO REIMBURSE YOU IN THE CURRENCY OF THIS DOCUMENTARY CREDIT IN ACCORDANCE WITH YOUR INSTRUCTIONS.

+NEGOTIATING BANK'S DISCOUNT AND/OR INTEREST, IF ANY , PRIOR TO REIMBURSEMENT BY US ARE FOR ACCOUNT OF BENEFICIARY.

+PLEASE ALSO STATE THE APPROPRIATE ABA NO. AND CHIPS UID ON YOUR COVERING SCHEDULE TO US.

Sender to Receiver Information	:72:+BENEFICIARY'S
	TEL: 0086-517-84917076
	CONTACT PERSON:LEON
Trailer	

Task 3 Requesting to Amend an L/C

Part I. Introduction

Upon receipt of the relevant L/C, the beneficiary (seller) of the L/C should, first of all, make a thorough examination to it to find whether the clauses in the L/C are in complete conformity with the terms in the contract. If any discrepancies occur, the beneficiary (seller) should ask the applicant (buyer) to ask for his issuing bank to amend the L/C accordingly.

Moreover, the applicant (buyer) may also ask for amendment.

The following points may be given for reference in the examination of L/C:

- Make sure whether the issuing bank is a sound reliable foreign bank or not, whether the currency employed and other reimbursement clauses are clear and in accordance with the regulations in the exporting country.

- The L/C should usually be irrevocable without any restrictions, such as "subject to import license obtainable", etc.
- Make sure whether the goods description (specifications, quantity, number, packing, marks, etc.)is in accordance with the sale contract.
- The total amount, validity time and date and place of expiry.
- Make sure whether the required documents (invoice, c/o, B/L, insurance policy, etc.)are in accordance with the sales contract.

Part II. Writing Skills

For letters amending an L/C:

Step 1: To thank the arrival of L/C.

主要是感谢对方开来的信用证并引出信用证的号码。

e.g. We are very pleased to receive your L/C No.025HGM356 issued by THE BANK OF TOKYO, LTD. NEW YORK AGENCY 100 BROADWAY NEW YORK, N.Y.10005, dated JUNE 15. 2002.

Thank you for your L/C No.MQC0278 established by ALAHLI BANK OF KUWAIT, dated 5 MAY 2002.

Step 2: To state the discrepancies between contract and L/C.

e.g. However we are sorry to find it contains the following discrepancies.

But the following points are in discrepancy with the stipulation of our S/C No.02CHES98.

Step 3: To ask for amendment to the L/C accordingly.

e.g. As to the description of the goods please insert the word…before… (有关货物的描述，请在……前插入……)

The… should be…, not …

The …should be… instead of …

Please delete the clause…

As there is no direct steamer sailing to your port next month, please amend the relative L/C to read "transshipment allowed".

Please extend the shipment date and the validity of the L/C to …and …respectively. (请分别把装运期和信用证有效期扩展到……和……)

Chapter 6 Terms of Payment

Step 4: To express the wish of receiving L/C amendment ASAP.（感谢对方的合作，提醒信用证修改书应于某日前到达，以便按时装运等。）

e.g. Thank you for your kind cooperation, please see to it that the L/C amendment reach us before××× (date), failing which we shall not be able to effect punctual shipment.

For letters extending an L/C:

Step 1: To mention the number of the L/C.

Step 2: To express regret being unable to conform to the stipulations of the L/C.

Step 3: To ask for extension.

Step 4: To show thanks and expectation of receiving the amendment.

Part III. Sample Letters

Sample 1   Asking for Amending an L/C

Simpson and Sons

54 Madison street Sydney

Australia

Dear sirs,

　　We have received your L/C No.5058 covering 200 dozen poplin shirts. On perusal, we have found some discrepancies which please amend as follow:

1. The beneficiary should be "The Pacific Trading Co., Ltd".

2. "Sight L/C" instead of "60 days L/C".

3. "CFRC3 Marseilles" instead of "CFR Marseilles".

4. The total value should be "US$ 300,000" but not "stg £300,000".

As the date of delivery is drawing near, we will appreciate your early amendment.

Thank you in advance for your cooperation.

　　　　　　　　　　　　　　　　　　　　　　Yours faithfully,

　　　　　　　　　　　　　　　　　　　　　　　　(signature)

Notes

1. discrepancy　　*n*. 相差，差异，矛盾

2. beneficiary　　*n*. 受益人

3. total value　　总值

4. date of delivery　　交货期

5. appreciate 感激

6. amendment 修改

   amend an L/C 修改信用证

   amendment to L/C 信用证修改书

Sample 2 Asking for Amending the Amount & Packing Terms

Dear Sirs,

   Re: L/C No. 345 issued by First National City Bank

   We have received the above L/C established by you in payment for your Order No.678 covering 200 cases of….

   When we checked the L/C with the relevant contract, we found that the amount in your L/C is insufficient. The correct total CIF New York value of your order comes to US$2,750.00 instead of US$ 2,550.00, the difference being US$ 200.00.

   Your L/C allows us only half a month to effect delivery. But when we signed the contract we have agreed that the delivery should be made within one month upon receipt of the letter of credit.

   As to packing, the contract stipulates that the goods should be packed in cartons and reinforced with nylon straps outside, but your L/C required metal straps instead. We think we should arrange the packing according to the contract.

   In view of the above, you are kindly requested to increase the amount of your L/C by US$200.00, extend the shipment and validity to September 15 and 30 respectively, as well as amend the term of packing. Meanwhile please advise us by fax.

                                  Yours faithfully,

                                      (signature)

Notes

1. insufficient *adj.* 不足的

   sufficient *adj.* 充足的，足够的

   e.g. The quantity you offered is insufficient for our requirements.

       你方所报数量不够我方的需求。

2. come to 达到，共计

   e.g. The net amount of compensation comes to US$10000 only.

       净赔偿金额共计10000美元。

Chapter 6　Terms of Payment

3. effect delivery　交货

4. sign the contract　签订合同

5. as to　关于

6. be packed in cartons　装在纸箱内

7. stipulate　*vt.* 规定

   stipulation　*n.* 规定，条款

8. reinforce　*vt.* 加固，加强

9. in view of　考虑到，鉴于

10. respectively　分别地

Sample 3　Asking for Transshipment and Partial Shipments

Dear Sirs,

　　Letter of Credit No.3524 issued by the Bank of New South Wales has duly arrived. On perusal, we find that transshipment and partial shipments are not allowed.

　　As direct steamers to your port are few and far between, we have to ship via Hong Kong more often than not. As to partial shipment, it would be to our mutual benefit if we could ship immediately whatever is ready instead of waiting for the whole shipment to be completed. Therefore, we are asking you to amend your L/C to read "partial shipments and transshipment allowed."

　　We shall appreciate it if you will modify promptly the L/C as requested.

　　　　　　　　　　　　　　　　　　　　　　　　　　Yours faithfully,

　　　　　　　　　　　　　　　　　　　　　　　　　　　(signature)

Notes

1. on perusal　在仔细（细读、详阅）之后

2. transshipment　转船，转运

   e.g. As there is no direct steamer to your port, please amend L/C to allow transshipment.
   因为没有驶往你港的直达轮船，请将信用证修改为允许转船。

3. partial shipments　分批装运

   partial　*adj.* 部分的

   e.g. We enclose a check in partial payment for the goods shipped on consignment.
   随函附寄支票一张，作为所装来的寄售货物的部分款项。

4. via *prep.* 经由(=by way of)

　　e.g. The goods will be shipped via Hong Kong.　货物将由香港转运。

　　　　The samples were sent via airmail.　样品已航寄。

per 和 ex 都是介词，在表示由什么货轮装运货物的时候是有区别的，per 主要表示由什么货轮运出，而 ex 是表示由什么货轮运进来。

　　e.g. We wish to inform you that the goods you ordered has been shipped per s.s. "Peace" today.

　　　　我们愿告知你方，你方所订货物已于今日由"和平"号轮运出。

　　　　We have received the goods shipped ex s.s. "Peace".

　　　　我们已收到了由"和平"号轮运来的货物。

5. more often than not　经常，多半(=very frequently)

6. mutual benefit　互利

7. modify　*vt.* 更改，修改

　　modify the terms of a contract　修改合同条款

Sample 4　Asking for Extension—the Sailing Date of the Ship is Later than Stipulated Time

Dear Sirs,

　　Re: Your L/C No.AG4582

　　We have received your L/C No.AG4582 for the amount of ￡2,960 to cover your Order No.860 for metric tons of frozen shrimp.

　　The said credit calls for shipment on or before the 31st of December. As the earliest steamer sailing for your port is S.S. "PEACE" scheduled to leave Shanghai on or about January 3 next year, it is therefore, impossible for us to effect shipment at the time you named.

　　This being the case, we have to ask you to extend the date of shipment to the 15th of January, under advice to us by fax.

　　　　　　　　　　　　　　　　　　　　　　Yours faithfully,

　　　　　　　　　　　　　　　　　　　　　　　(signature)

Notes

1. S.S. "PEACE" 和平号轮船　S.S. 为 steam ship 缩写，后面跟船名

　　e.g. Please be informed that we have shipped the goods by s.s. "Victoria".

　　　　兹通知贵方我们已经将货物装上了"维多利亚"号轮。

　　M.V.　motor vessel 的缩写，后面跟船名

Chapter 6 Terms of Payment

e.g. We have loaded the goods on M.V. "Peace".

2. effect shipment   即 make shipment 或 ship，装船

   effect delivery   即 make delivery 或 deliver，交货

   effect insurance   即 make insurance 或 insure，投保

3. this being the case   事实既然如此

   还可以说：such (that) being the case

4. extend   *vt.* 延期，延长

   e.g. extend the deadline until the end of the month   展期到月底截止。

   extension   *n.* 延长，延期

   e.g. the extension of a contract   合同有效期的延长

5. under advice to sb   并通知某人

Sample 5   Asking for Extension—Goods Are Not Ready

Dear Sirs,

L/C No. DCTAO910536-1000 sets electric fans

We thank you for your L/C No. DCTAO910536 for the captioned goods. We are sorry that owing to some delay on the part of our suppliers, we are unable to get the goods ready before the end of this month. So we write to you asking for an extension.

It is expected that the consignment will be ready for shipment in the early part of May and we are arranging to ship it on S.S. "Red Star" sailing from Shanghai on May 10.

We are looking forward to receiving your extension of the above L/C, thus enabling us to effect shipment of goods in question.

Yours faithfully,

(signature)

Notes

1. captioned goods   标题项下的货物
2. owing to   由于
3. consignment   货物
4. in question   正在考虑到的，正在讨论的，该，所涉及的

   e.g. The goods in question have been in good demand since the beginning of this year.

   自本年初以来该货一直畅销。

Sample 6　Amendment to an L/C

INDUSTRIAL AND COMMERCIAL BANK OF CHINA

ADVICE OF AMENDMENT　　　　　　　HUAIAN BRANCH

信用证修改通知书　　　　　　81 WEST HUAIAN ROAD HUAIAN CHINA

　　　　　　　　　　　　　　　　　　TEL: (0086)517-83915111

　　　　　　　　　　　　　　　　　　FAX: (0086)517-83937158

　　　　　　　　　　　　　　　　　　SWIFT BIC: ICBKCNBJHYC

TO（致）：　　　　　　　　　　　EMAIL: INTL-HA@JSJCBC.COM.CN

淮安市利润对外贸易有限公司　　　　**DATE**（日期）：4. JUNE 2009

OUR REF NO.（我行通知编号）：AV061050900131　　（PLEASE ALWAYS QUOTE）

L/C NO.（信用证号）：DCTAO910536

DATE OF ISSUE（开证日）：15. APRIL 2009

ISSUER（开证方）：HONGKONG AND SHANGHAI BANKING CORPORATION LIMITED, THE TAIPEI, CHINA

ORIGINAL AMOUNT（原始金额）：USD3766608

AMENDMENT AMOUNT（本次修改金额）：USD 57600

L/C LATEST AMOUNT（信用证最新金额）：USD 3709008

AMENDMENT NO.（修改次数）：1

DATE OF AMENDMENT（修改日）：2009.06.04

DEAR SIRS（敬启者），

WE HAVE PLEASURE IN ADVISING YOU THAT WE HAVE RECEIVED FROM THE A/M BANK AN AMENDMENT TO THE CAPTION ED L/C. CONTENTS OF WHICH ARE AS PER ATTACHED SHEET(S).

兹通知贵司，我行收到上述银行信用证修改一份，内容见附件。

PLEASE NOTE THAT THIS ADVICE DOES NOT CONSTITUTE OUR CONFIRMATION OF ABOVE AMENDMENT.

本通知不构成我行对上述信用证修改的保兑。

THIS AMENDMENT SHOULD BE ATTACHED TO THE CAPTIONED L/C ADVISED BY US, OTHERWISE. THE BENEFICIARY WILLBE REPONSIBLE FOR ANY CORESPONDENCE ARISING THEREFROM.

Chapter 6 Terms of Payment

本修改须抚育有关信用证，否则，贵司须对因此而产生的后果承担责任。

适用规则：SUBJECT TO UCP LATEST VERSION

IF YOU HAVE ANY FURTHER QUERIES, PLEASE DON'T HESTATE TO CONTACT US ON THE ABOVE MENTIONED NUMBER.

如果贵司有任何疑问，请按上述业务编号与我行联系。

THIS IS A COMPUTER-GENERATED LETTER, NO SIGNATURE REQUIRED.

本函由计算机生成，无需签字。

Formatted incoming SWIFT message MT	
Own BIC/TID	:II: ICBKCNBJJSP BIC identified as: INDUSTRIAL AND COMMERCIAL BANK OF CHINA, JIANGSU PROVINCIAL BRANCH 404, ZHONGSHAN ROAD EAST 210002 NANJING, China
SWIFT Message Type	:MT 707 Amendments to a Documentary Credit
Correspondents BIC/TID	:IO HSBCTWTPOBU BIC resolved to different Department HSBCTWTPCBS HONGKONG AND SHANGHAI BANKING CORPORATION LIMITED, China
Sender's Reference	:20: DC TA0910536
Receiver's Reference	:21: NONREF
Date of Issue	:31C:2009.04.15
Date of Amendment	:30:2009.06.04
Number of Amendment	:26E:01
Beneficiary (Before This Amendment)	:59: HUAIAN LIRUN FOREIGN TRADE CO., LTD. HUAIAN 23 EAST BEIJING ROAD, HUAIYIN DISTRICT, HUAIAN CITY JIANGSU 223300, CHINA
Decrease of Documentary Credit Amount	:33B: USD 576.00
New Documentary Credit	:34B USD 37090.08

```
Amount after Amendment
Narrative Description of the                    :79:
Original Message
    GOODS
DELETE:
CHRISTMAS DECORATION 24,216 ……PER PO
S9CCE06901
INSERT:
CHRISTMAS DECORATION
22,296 PCS, DETALL PER PO S9CCE06901
ADDITIONAL CONDITIONS
INSERT:
+THIS DC AMENDMENT IS SUBJECT TO THE BENEFICIARY'S
CONSENT, PLEASE URGENTLY OBTAIN THEIR CONSENT AND
ADVISE US VIA SWIFT QUOTING THE ABOVE DC NO.
Trailer
```

Part IV. Useful Expressions and Typical Sentences

Useful Expressions

1. letter of credit/credit 信用证
2. confirming bank 保兑行
3. documentary credit 跟单信用证
4. negotiating bank 议付行
5. reimbursing bank 偿付行
6. nominated bank 指定银行
7. revocable 可撤销的
8. applicant 开证申请人
9. irrevocable 不可撤销的
10. beneficiary 受益人
11. confirmed 保兑的
12. application 开证申请书
13. unconfirmed 不保兑的
14. L/C amendment 信用改证书
15. negotiation 议付
16. terms and conditions 条款
17. acceptance 承兑
18. undertake/engage/guarantee 保证
19. issuing/opening/establishing bank 开证行
20. present 提示
21. advising bank 通知行
22. test key 密押
23. uniform customs and practice for documentary credits/UCP 跟单信用证统一惯例

Chapter 6 Terms of Payment

24. period of validity   有效期

25. expiry date of credit   信用证到期日

26. mode of transport and route   运输方式和路线

27. insurance cover   承保范围

28. delivery terms   交付条款

29. transferable credit   可转让信用证

30. back to back credit   对背信用证

31. authenticated by test telex   用加押电传证实

32. absolute or in strict conformity/strict compliance   严格相符

33. similar credit   套证

34. apparent authenticity   表面上的真实性

35. mail confirmation   邮寄证实书

36. details to follow   详情后告

37. amendment to the credit   信用证修改书

38. discrepancy/defect   不符点

39. waiver of the discrepancy   接受不符点

40. credit line   信用额度

41. ocean bill of lading   海运提单

42. endorsed in blank/blank endorsement   空白背书

43. marked freight prepaid   标明运费已付

44. latest shipping date/latest date for shipment   最晚装运日

45. the first following business day   下一个银行工作日

46. bearer documents   不记名单据

47. proceed with the import formalities   办理进口手续

48. appear on their face   表面看来

49. packing credit   打包贷款

50. post-import finance   进口押汇

51. trust receipt   信托收据

52. international division of advising bank   通知行的国际业务部

53. operative   生效

54. notice of dishonor   拒付通知

Typical Sentences

Useful Sentences for Negotiating Terms of Payment

1. We usually accept payment by irrevocable L/C payable against shipping documents.

2. We cannot accept L/C available by draft at 60 days' sight.

3. We would appreciate it very much if you can accept payment by D/P at 30 days' sight.

4. In compliance with your request, we exceptionally advance shipment and accept payment against D/P at sight.

5. For payment, we require 100% value, confirmed and irrevocable letter of credit with partial shipment and transshipment allowed clause, available by draft at sight, payable against surrendering the full set of shipping documents to the negotiating bank here.

Useful Sentences for Urging Establishment of an L/C

1. Please arrange for the establishing of an irrevocable L/C in our favor.

2. Please do your utmost to rush the L/C establishment so that we can execute the contract smoothly.

3. As the amount of our Order No. 11 is below US $1000, please agree to payment by D/P because an L/C will cost us much.

4. Emphasis has to be laid on the point that the L/C must reach us before May 1.

5. In order to avoid subsequent amendments, please see to it that the L/C stipulations are in exact conformity with the terms and conditions of the S/C 168.

6. Please open the L/C in exact accordance with the clauses of S/C 888 ASAP to avoid future amendment.

7. This L/C will remain valid until Mar. 8, 2008, confirmed by Bank of China, Hangzhou branch.

8. Payment is to be made against sight draft drawn under a confirmed, irrevocable letter of credit without recourse.

9. In compliance with your request, we exceptionally accept payment against D/P at sight.

10. Your compliance with our request will be highly appreciated.

11. We are awaiting the arrival of your L/C, on receipt of which we shall make the shipment of your order.

12. We have opened a letter of credit with ABC Bank in your favor, for US$1000000, covering your order No. 22, available until April 15.

Chapter 6 Terms of Payment

Useful Sentences for Amending an L/C

1. Thank you for your L/C NO.xxx for the amount of US$6000 covering 500 pieces of Canvas Folding Chairs with wooden frame.

2. On perusal, we find that…

3. We would, therefore, be compelled to ask you to amend your L/C to read "partial shipment and transshipment allowed".

4. We shall appreciate it very much if you will amend your L/C without delay.

5. Please insert the word "on or about" before the time of shipment in L/C No.6889.

6. Upon checking L/C No.5578 for S/C No.123, we regret to find that the unit price is US$3.25 as contracted.

7. The amount in your L/C is short opened US$ 500, please increase as stipulated in the contract.

8. Regarding L/C No 6523, we will appreciate it if you will instruct the bank to amend the commission as 5%.

9. In order to avoid subsequent amendments, please see to it that the L/C stipulations are in exact accordance with the terms of S/C.

10. Please delete the clause "Transshipment at HK prohibited" from your L/C.

Part V. Project Training

Project 1

Training Situation:

A foreign client from Australia has ordered US$10000 worth of energy saving spark plug from the exporter. He does not accept sight L/C just like the first business and suggests paying by T/T within 15 days after receiving B/L for his imports this time and tries to persuade the exporter to accept T/T terms.

Training Requirements:

Students as clients (buyers) are requested to practice writing a letter asking for payment by T/T.

Hints:

1. Opening an L/C will cost buyers a lot.
2. It is not the first order between them.

3. It is not a large order.

Project 2

Training Situation:

Mr. Green from America has decided to purchase 50 metric tons of groundnut kernels from China. He has settled the price and quantity, but the mode of payment has not been discussed. He faxed to Mr. Li, a representative of China National Cereals, Oils and Foodstuffs Import & Export Corporation to suggest payment by D/P.

Training Requirements:

1. Why does Mr. Green suggest paying by D/P?
2. How does Mr. Wang reply him?
3. Write a letter to persuade Mr. Wang to accept Mr. Green's opinion.

Project 3

Training Situation I:

Mr. Smith from New York decides to purchase Chinese Cotton Piece Goods from China. He has settled the price, quantity and shipment date. As to the mode of payment, he faxed to Mr. Sun, a representative of China National Textiles Import & Export Corporation suggesting payment on D/A basis.

Training Requirements:

1. Why does Mr. Smith suggest paying by D/A?
2. What about Mr. Sun's opinion?
3. Write an outline as Mr. Sun to insist on paying by L/C.

Training Situation II:

Mr. Smith has not agreed to make payment by L/C as opening an L/C will cost him a lot and tie up funds. He hopes this time Mr. Sun will accommodate him by accepting D/A, but Mr. Sun insists on paying by L/C.

Training Requirements:

Students act as sellers to write a letter declining Mr. Smith.

Chapter 6 Terms of Payment

Project 4

Training Situation:

信用证存在问题	应该如何修改	要求修改理由
信用证大小写金额不一致	NINE HUNDRED AND EIGHTY ONLY	金额低于合同金额
信用证在国外到期	FOR NEGOTIATION IN BENEFICIARY COUNTRY	国外到期易产生逾期
保险金额过高	FOR 110% OF INVOICE VALUE	投保金额超出合同规定
保险险别错误	WPA CLASH & BREAKAGE, WAR RISKS AS PER	应根据合同规定投保
证明装运货物数量有误	HX1115 542 SETS HX4510 254 SETS	装运数量多于合同规定
目的港有误	SHIPMENT FROM SHANGHAI TO TORONTO	目的港应与合同相符
禁止转运	TRANSSHIPMENT PERMITTED	合同明确规定允许转运
集装箱数与实际不符	SHIPPED IN FOUR 20' CY TO CY CONTAINERS	一个20英尺箱装不下

Training Requirements:

According to the above amendment requirements, please write a letter for amending the letter of credit.

Project 5

Training Situation:

Erie Confectionery & Bakery, Ltd. has received the fax from Ruihua Native Produce & Animal by-Products Company asking for extension of the L/C to June 30th and July 15th for shipment and negotiation respectively. But the selling season is coming. Shipment in June will inevitably cause him heavy losses.

Training Requirements:

Write a letter to Ruihua Native Produce & Animal by-Products Company rejecting L/C extension.

Part VI. Optional Study

I. Related Information

1. Swift Company Information

SWIFT is the Society for Worldwide Interbank Financial Telecommunication, a member-owned cooperative through which the financial world conducts its business operations with speed, certainty and confidence. Over 8300 banking organizations, securities institutions and corporate customers in more than 208 countries trust us every day to exchange millions of standardized financial messages.

Our role is two-fold. We provide the proprietary communications platform, products and services that allow our customers to connect and exchange financial information securely and reliably. We also act as the catalyst that brings the financial community together to work collaboratively to shape market practice, define standards and consider solutions to issues of mutual interest.

SWIFT enables its customers to automate and standardize financial transactions, thereby lowering costs, reducing operational risk and eliminating inefficiencies from their operations. By using SWIFT customers can also create new business opportunities and revenue streams.

SWIFT has its headquarters in Belgium and has offices in the world's major financial centres and developing markets.

SWIFT is solely a carrier of messages. It does not hold funds nor does it manage accounts on behalf of customers, nor does it store financial information on an on-going basis. As a data carrier, SWIFT transports messages between two financial institutions. This activity involves the secure exchange of proprietary data while ensuring its confidentiality and integrity.

2. L/C Application Form

IRREVOCABLE DOCUMENTARY CREDIT APPLICATION

TO: BANK OF CHINA BEIJING BRANCH	Date:
☐Issue by airmail ☐With brief advice by teletransmission ☐Issue by express delivery ☐Issue by teletransmission (which shall be the operative instrument)	Credit No. Date and place of expiry
Applicant	Beneficiary (Full name and address)

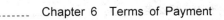 Chapter 6 Terms of Payment

Advising Bank	Amount
Partial shipments ☐allowed ☐not allowed	Transshipment ☐allowed ☐not allowed	Credit available with By

| Loading on board/dispatch/taking in charge at/from

not later than
For transportation to:
☐FOB   ☐CFR   ☐CIF
☐or other terms | ☐sight payment   ☐acceptance
☐negotiation
☐deferred payment at / against the documents detailed herein
☐and beneficiary's draft(s) for _____ % of invoice value at_____ sight drawn on |

Documents required: (marked with X)
1. (   ) Signed commercial invoice in _____ copies indicating L/C No. and Contract No.
2. (   ) Full set of clean on board Bills of Lading made out to order and blank endorsed, marked "freight [   ] to collect / [   ]prepaid [   ] showing freight amount" notifying _____ .
(   ) Airway bills/cargo receipt/copy of railway bills issued by _____ showing "freight [   ] to collect/[   ] prepaid [   ] indicating freight amount" and consigned to_____.
3. (   ) Insurance Policy/Certificate in _____ copies for _____ % of the invoice value showing claims payable in in currency of the draft, blank endorsed, covering All Risks, War Risks and _____ .
4. (   ) Packing List/Weight Memo in _____ copies indicating quantity, gross and weights of each package.
5. (   ) Certificate of Quantity/Weight in _____ copies issued by _____ .
6. (   ) Certificate of Quality in _____ copies issued by [   ] manufacturer/[   ] public recognized surveyor_____ .
7. (   ) Certificate of Origin in _____ copies .
8. (   ) Beneficiary's certified copy of fax / telex dispatched to the applicant within _____ days after shipment advising L/C No., name of vessel, date of shipment, name, quantity, weight and value of goods.

Other documents, if any

Description of goods:

Additional instructions:
1. (   ) All banking charges outside the opening bank are for beneficiary's account.
2. (   ) Documents must be presented within ____ days after date of issuance of the transport documents but within the validity of this credit.
3. (   ) Third party as shipper is not acceptable, Short Form/Blank back B/L is not acceptable.
4. (   ) Both quantity and credit amount _____ % more or less are allowed.
5. (   ) All documents must be sent to issuing bank by courier/speed post in one lot.
   (   ) Other terms, if any

II. Supplementary Specimen Letters

Specimen Letter 1

Dear Sirs,

We have received your statement for the quarter ended September 30 and found that it agrees with our books. As requested, we have instructed our banks to send the sum of US$5000.00 by T/T for the credit of your account at the bank of China, Beijing Branch.

This payment clears your account up to August 31. The unpaid balance of US$ 2,000.00 for the goods supplied during September will be telegraphed by our bankers on or before November 15.

Yours faithfully,

(signature)

Specimen Letter 2

Dear Sirs,

Our Sales Confirmation No.TE151

With reference to the 4,000 dozen shirts under Sales Confirmation No.Te151, we wish to draw your attention to the fact that the date of delivery is approaching, but up to the present we have not received the covering Letter of Credit. Please do your utmost to expedite its establishment, so that we may execute the order within the prescribed time.

In order to avoid subsequent amendment, please see to it that the L/C stipulations are in exact accordance with the terms of the contract.

We look forward to receiving your favorable response at an early date.

Yours faithfully,

(signature)

Specimen Letter 3

Dear Mr. Metron,

Thank you for your letter of November 11, 2001.

We have considered your request for a trial delivery of China on documents against acceptance terms, but regret to say that we cannot agree to your proposal.

As an exception, the best we can do for the trial is to offer you direct payment at sight terms.

Chapter 6 Terms of Payment

> If you accept our proposal, you run very little risk, since our company is well known for its high quality, attractive design and reasonable price. Our lines sell very well all over the world and have done so far for the last 50 years. We do not think you will have any difficulties in achieving a satisfactory volume of sales.
>
> If you find our proposal acceptable, please let us know and we can then expedite the transaction.
>
> Yours faithfully,
(signature)

Part VII. Exercises

I. Answer the following questions:

1. How many main terms of payment are there in foreign trade?
2. State the three forms of "remittance".
3. What is the most popular method used in foreign trade?
4. Why is L/C commonly used in foreign trade?
5. How many forms of "collection" are there in foreign trade?
6. On receipt of the relative L/C what should the seller do first?
7. If the terms in the L/C and the relative contract are different from each other, what should the seller do?
8. What is the usual procedure for the seller to ask for making amendment?

II. Translate the following terms and expressions:

A. Into Chinese:

1. Letter of Credit
2. the establishment of L/C
3. documentary L/C
4. issuing bank
5. paying bank
6. applicant
7. beneficiary
8. L/C at sight
9. the confirmed L/C
10. an irrevocable L/C payable at sight
11. the matter in question
12. We are not in a position to open the covering L/C owing to the strike here.
13. extend the time of shipment
14. owing to
15. in conformity with
16. discrepancy

17. in view of 18. draw one's attention to

19. Please amend the name of commodity in L/C.

20. brisk demand

B. Into English:

1. 信用证修改书   2. 执行订单

3. 合同展期   4. 有效期

5. 加快装运   6. 以某人为受益人

7. 兹谈及   8. 经详阅

III. Choose the best answer to complete each of the following sentences:

1. Your request for payment _____ Letter of Credit is unacceptable.
   A. with   B. by   C. using   D. of

2. The L/C established by you through the Bank of China will____ at the end of this month.
   A. due   B. be due   C. mature   D. expire

3. As instructed, we will draw_____ you a sight draft for collection through the Bank of China.
   A. for   B. against   C. on   D. from

4. We will instruct our bank to issue an L/C____ favor of your company.
   A. on   B. for   C. with   D. in

5. We_____ that your failure to open the covering L/C is due to the financial trouble on your side.
   A. aware   B. are aware   C. see   D. are to aware

6. We regret_____ unable to accept your terms of payment as mentioned in your last mail.
   A. to be   B. being   C. to   D. for being

7. The goods will be _____ to breakage if you do not pack them in cartons.
   A. get   B. suffered   C. subject   D. subjected

8. We have instructed the bank to ____ the amendment you ask for.
   A. perform   B. fulfill   C. effect   D. do

9. If a draft is attached ____ shipping documents, it is a documentary draft.
   A. to   B. on   C. of   D. with

10. Please send us the amendment_____ L/C immediately or we shall not be able to ship your order on time.
    A. of   B. to   C. as to   D. with

Chapter 6 Terms of Payment

11. We wish to_____ your attention to the fact your L/C amount is insufficient to cover the goods under S/C No. 896.

  A. have   B. get   C. call   D. obtain

12. The quality of your last shipment is not_____ conformity with that of your sample.

  A. of   B. on   C. to   D. in

IV. Supply the missing words in the blanks of the following letter. The first letters are given:

> Dear Sirs,
>
>   We thank you f_____ your o_____ No.905 for 50 metric tons of Emery Powder but r____ being u_____ to accept your terms of payment mentioned therein.
>
>   In our last letter we sent you our specimen contract in which are contained the general sales terms and conditions. If you have gone through the specimen contract you will see that our u_____ terms of payment are by c_____, i_____ letter of credit in our favor, available by draft at sight, reaching us one month ahead of shipment, r_____ valid for n_____ in China till the 21st day after the p_____ time of shipment, and a_____ transshipment and partial shipments.
>
>   We also mentioned in our letter of 14th June that several big Italian firms had already d_____ business with us according to the above terms so as to get the first transaction c_____.
>
>   As soon as we hear from you in the affirmative we will send you the contract so that the goods can be ready for shipment as r_____.
>
>   We look forward to r_____ your favorable reply soon.
>
>   Yours faithfully,
>
>   China National Import & Export Corp.

V. Translate the following sentences into English:

1. 因第 EX112 号销售合同项下的货物已备妥待运，请尽快敦促开证。
2. 如你方承诺早一个月安排装运，我方将开立信用证。
3. 我方从你方 12 月 19 日的传真获悉，信用证已开出，但我方仍未收到银行的通知。
4. 遗憾的是我方不断敦促客户开立信用证但没有成功。
5. 按惯例我方要求即期信用证付款，因此对这次交易我方无法破例。

6．由于开立信用证有困难，客户要求你方接受以电汇方式支付。

7．我方发现你方信用证的条款与合同不符。

8．请按合同价格尽快开立信用证，否则我方无法申请出口许可证。

9．信用证 345 号，请修改如下：

（1）长吨改为公吨

（2）目的港伦敦改为汉堡

（3）展装运期到 8 月底，并允许分运转船

10．你方信用证 3350 号，数量与合同不符，总金额相差£75.60，请速修改。

11．信用证 3346 号，金额不足，请按合同增加 520 镑（请按合同增至 3125.00 镑）。

12．请将你方信用证 6789 号的船期及有效期分别延展至 10 月 15 日及 10 月 30 日。

13．收到你公司对第××号售货确认书开出的第××号信用证。经核对来证条款，发现来证单价为 US$3.25，而合约单价是 US$3.52。估计系书写笔误，请予修改。

VI. Write a letter with the following particulars:

1．11 月 12 日来函收到，获悉你方有意在贵国推销我们的自行车。对此我们非常感兴趣。

2．对你方为推销自行车所做的努力我们甚为感激。

3．但对你方要求以见票后 60 天付款交单方式付款一事，我们歉难考虑。

4．我们的通常做法是要求即期信用证付款。

5．为了促进我方自行车在贵方市场上的销售，我方准备接受即期付款交单方式，以示特别照顾。希望你方能接受上述付款条件并盼早日收到回音。

Chapter 7

Packing

Task 1 Informing Packing Requirements

Part I. Introduction

1. On packing

Packing is of great importance in foreign trade. Packing is an art. It needs more care in export trade than in home trade. Packing can keep the goods safe and complete and prevent loss and leakage in their whole circulation, and it can raise its value and promote the sales. Generally speaking, there are two forms of packing: (1) large packing/outer packing, i.e., packing for transportation; (2) small packing/inner packing, i.e., sales packing.

2. The Indispensable Contents Required in a Packing Clause

A packing clause is an integral part of a sales contract or a Letter of Credit. Generally, the following contents are required in the packing clause:

(1) who is to bear the packing cost: the seller or the buyer

(2) the method of packing: cases, bales, barrels, baskets or containers, etc.

(3) the packing specification: the quantity in each unit, the dimension of the package, etc.

(4) the marking on the outer packing

3. The Role of a Packing List

Responding to the requirements of some buyers, the exporter needs to issue a packing list to confirm the detailed information of the shipment of cargo exported. From the packing list, the buyer and the carrier can determine in how many packages the whole lot is packed and the particular items in each package. We can also regard a packing list as a more specific version of a commercial invoice without price information.

When required by some nations and buyers, the packing list is attached to the outside of each container of the lot of goods in a waterproof envelope marked "Packing List" or "Packing List Enclosed" for check by authorities of both the exporter and importer countries. It is not necessary to have the packing list in every deal, it will depend on the nature of the goods in the definite business. Usually business of bulk goods, such as agricultural products, or chemicals, weight memo will be needed. A packing list is often one of the required documents that the exporter should submit to the bank for negotiation under the payment method of L/C.

Chapter 7 Packing

Generally, letters about packing issues should be concise and clear. In such letters, the seller can describe in detail to the buyer his customary packing of the goods concerned and also indicate clearly that he may accept any required packing at the expense of the buyer.

Part II. Writing Skills

For letters informing packing requirements:

包装要求信函的结构如下：

1. 表达写信意图。(expressing the purpose of the letter, i.e., offering packing requirements)
2. 指定包装要求。(specifying the packing requirements)
3. 表明期望。(indicating your expectation and desire)

Part III. Sample Letters

Sample 1 Buyer's Packing Requirements

Dear Sirs,

Thank you for your quotation of March 15th. We are working on it and expect to come to a decision in about a fortnight.

As specified in our inquiry of March 10th, and also in our follow-up letter of the same date, the goods should be packed in seaworthy cases suitable for a long voyage and well protected against dampness, shock, and rough handling. The seller should be liable for any damages to the goods and extra expenses due to improper packing and inadequate protective measures.

When you pack the goods, please see to it that the package number, measurement, gross weight, net weight, the words "KEEP AWAY FROM MOISTURE", and the following shipping mark shall be printed with fadeless paint on each package:

SIPC/TITC26V-400ZC

Upon receipt of the letter, please confirm by fax that you will fulfil these packing instructions.

Yours faithfully,

(signature)

Notes

1. follow-up *adj.* 后续的，接着的

   a follow-up letter 后续信函

a follow-up visit   继续访问

2. rough handling   粗鲁搬运，野蛮装卸

e.g. Considering this damage was due to the rough handling by the steamship company, we claimed on them for recovery of the loss.

考虑到这些损失是由于船运公司的野蛮装卸引起的，我们向他们提出索赔。

3. see to it that…   请注意，确保，务必

e.g. Pease see to it that our terms of payment are by irrevocable L/C.

请注意我们的付款方式是以不可撤消的信用证支付。

4. fulfil   *v.* 完成

e.g. We'll fulfil your order in the near future.

我们不久将完成你方订单。

Sample 2   Requirements for Packing and Marking

Dear Sirs,

We acknowledge receipt of your letter dated 9th this month enclosing the above sales contract in duplicate, but wish to state that after going through the contract, we find that the packing clause in it is not clear enough. The relative clause reads as follows: "Packing: Seaworthy export packing, suitable for long distance ocean transportation".

In order to eliminate possible future trouble, we should like to make clear beforehand our packing requirements as follows:

The tea under the captioned contract should be packed in international standard tin boxes, 24 boxes to a pallet, 10 pallets in an FCL container. On the outer packing please mark our initials KRC in a diamond, under which the port of destination and our order number should be stenciled. In addition, warning marks like KEEP DRY, USE NO HOOK, etc. should also be indicated.

We have made a footnote on the contract to that effect and are returning herein one copy of the contract after duly counter-signing it. We hope you will find it in order and pay special attention to the packing.

We look forward to receiving your shipping advice and thank you in advance.

Yours faithfully,

(signature)

Chapter 7 Packing

Notes

1. eliminate   *v.* 排除，剔除
2. pallet   *n.* 托盘，小货盘
3. use no hook   切勿用钩
4. footnote   *n.* 脚注/*v.* 在文件、书页上加脚注或附注

Sample 3 Offering Packing Requirements

Dear Sirs,

On May 20, we received your consignment of 40 cardboard cartons of steel screws.

We regret to inform you that 10 cartons were delivered damaged and the contents had spoiled, leading to some losses.

We accept that the damage was not your fault but feel that we must modify our packing requirements to avoid future losses.

We require that future packing be in wooden boxes of 20 kilos net, each wooden box containing 40 cardboard packs of 500 grams net.

Please let us know whether these specifications can be met by you and whether they will lead to an increase in your prices.

We look forward to your early confirmation.

Yours faithfully,

(signature)

Notes

1. content   *n.* 内装货物
2. modify our packing requirements   修改我们的包装要求
3. cardboard   薄纸板

Task 2   Reply to Packing Issues

Part I. Introduction

Generally speaking, there are three types of packing mark, i.e., shipping mark, indicative mark and warning mark.

Shipping mark is made up of a few simple geometric figures, letters, numbers or words. In most cases, it is written or pressed on top or sides of the container being shipped, and it is so designed that the consigner or the consignee can identify the goods easily. The purpose of using shipping mark is for easy identification, for saving time in doing formalities or making documents, and for keeping secret on the part of the consigner and the consignee because only the consigner and the consignee know the goods while others not.

The major component parts of a shipping mark can be illustrated as follows:

1. code of the consignee: usually represented by geometric figures such as triangle, rhombus, or circular.

2. code of the consigner: usually being English letters either in or out of the geometric figure.

3. number of the contract or the L/C.

4. the port of destination.

5. number of the commodity: sequence number or the total number of items inside.

and sometimes weight and dimensions.

Basically, the golden rule is to keep shipping marks as simple as possible as shown below:

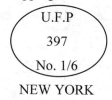

NEW YORK

U.F.P— initials of the importing/ exporting company

397— customer's order/ contract number

No. 1/6— case No. 1 of a consignment of 6 cases

NEW YORK— port of destination

Indicative mark is mainly used on goods which are easy to break or change their quantities on account of careless handling. They are usually made of eye-catching figures and words strategically painted or stenciled on the package so that the transporter can handle the goods accordingly.

小心轻放
Handle with care

防潮
Keep it out of water (rain)

Chapter 7   Packing

由此吊起
Lift from here

重心点
Gravitation here (Keep it in balance)

防热 (Away from heat)

远离热源 (Keep away from heat)

此端向上 (This side up)

防冻 (Keep it warm)

切勿用钩 (Use no hooks)

注意平放 (Keep flat (Stow level))

Warning mark is used for goods which are combustible (易燃的), explosive (易爆的), poisonous (有毒的), corrosive (腐蚀的), and radioactive (辐射性的).

Part II. Writing Skills

For letters in reply to the packing issues:

1. 对来信表达谢意。(expressing your thanks for the coming letter)

2. 表明你方的决定：接受或是不接受该包装。(indicating your decision: do or do not accept such packing)

3. 表述你方新的建议或解决办法。(expressing your new suggestions or solutions)

4. 邀请另一方对包装事宜予以确认。(inviting the confirmation on packing from the opposite party)

Part III. Sample Letters

Sample 1   Reply to Seller's Packing Clause

Dear Sirs,

　　Thank you for your supplementary ideas on the packing clause. We accept all of them and we would like to make an additional request based on what you have already offered.

　　As to the shipping mark, could you also mark, under our initials, the name of the port of destination as well as our order number in the same diamond? In addition, it will be highly appreciated if some indicative words like WATERPROOF can be marked on the surface of the cartons.

　　We look forward to your confirmation.

　　　　　　　　　　　　　　　　　　　　　　　　　　Yours faithfully,

　　　　　　　　　　　　　　　　　　　　　　　　　　　(signature)

Notes

1. packing clause　包装条款

2. shipping mark　运输标志，装运标志，唛头

3. 在正常语序中"under our initials"作为表方位的状语一般放在全句最后的"in the same diamond"短语的前面，本句中把它提前到目前的位置是出于两点考虑：其一，强调运输标志（即 shipping mark）上准备新添加的内容（即目的港名称和订单号码）具体该刷在哪里；其二，使行文的节奏有变化，增强可读性。

4. diamond　*n.* 金刚钻，钻石，菱形

5. indicative　*adj.* 指示的，预示的，暗示的

Sample 2　Reply to Seller's Proposal of Carton Packing

Dear Sirs,

　　With reference to your proposal of carton packing, we fully understand your reasons for such a change.

　　We have different experiences in terms of getting indemnification from the insurance company. According to you, the carton packing aids in pilferage revelation and thus helps to get compensation from insurance companies. However, we were confronted with a difficult dispute when we were in a claim two years ago when we were informed that the cartons were not seaworthy.

　　In this case, we would like to settle the packing issue in this way. When you export under CIF term, carton packing is allowed, but under FOB term, wooden cases are still used.

　　We are awaiting your further comments.

　　　　　　　　　　　　　　　　　　　　　　　　Yours faithfully,
　　　　　　　　　　　　　　　　　　　　　　　　(signature)

Notes

1. with reference to　关于

2. in terms of　就……而言，从……方面说来；根据，依据

3. indemnification　*n.* 赔偿；赔偿物（或赔偿金）

4. pilferage revelation 指"显示偷盗的痕迹"。因为纸板箱若被盗贼划开，留下的痕迹较木箱等其他包装工具更明显，若货主投保了"偷窃、提货不着险"的话，其索赔较容易被保险公司接受。

5. be confronted with　面临着

Sample 3　Reply to Instructions of Packing

July 21st, 2006

Dear Mr. Yang,

　　Re: Packing for Ready-made Garments

We thank you for your letter of July 17th, 2006 informing us of your clients' comments on our packing. We have discussed the matter with the competent department here and wish to explain as follows:

　　1. The cartons we use are up to standard and fit for ocean transportation. For years we have used these cartons in our shipments to many continental ports to the entire satisfaction of our clients. Moreover, the insurance companies have accepted such packing for WPA and TPND.

　　2. These cartons are well protected against moisture by plastic lining. Thus garments packed in them are not susceptible to damage by moisture as those packed in wooden cases.

　　3. The cardboard used for making cartons is light but compact. It keeps down packaging costs and helps customers save on freight.

　　4. Your clients' anxieties over packing are presumed. We are confident that the insurance company can be made to pay the necessary compensation for any loss or losses from pilferage and breakage caused by using such cartons.

　　Please tell your clients that their fears are unwarranted. Nowadays, except for bulk cargo, nude cargo and huge machinery, most commodities are packed in cartons. To pack garments in wooden cases is obsolete.

　　We highly value your comments, which will help improve our work. If you find any defect in our last shipment, please do not hesitate to let us know. We assure you of our cooperation and await your further orders.

　　Yours sincerely,

Wang Gang

General Manager

Notes

1. ready-made　*adj*. 现成的
2. competent　*adj*. 有能力的，胜任的
3. up to standard　符合标准，达到标准

4. to the entire satisfaction of sb.　令某人完全满意

5. lining　*n*. 衬里，里子；衬料，内衬

6. susceptible　*adj*. 易受影响的

7. compact　*adj*. 紧密的

8. presumed　*adj*. 假定的，推测的

9. unwarranted　*adj*. 没有根据的，无正当理由的；无保证的，未经保证的

10. bulk cargo　散装货

    nude cargo　裸装货

11. obsolete　*adj*. 已不用的，已废弃的，过时的

Part IV. Useful Expressions and Typical Sentences

Useful Expressions

1. in FCL (Full Container Load) container　用整集装箱装运

2. waterproof and airtight　防水且不漏气的

3. seaworthy export packing　适于海运的出口包装

4. inner/sales packing　内包装

5. outer/transportation packing　外包装

6. green packing　绿色/环保包装

7. shipping mark　运输标志

8. indicative mark　指示性标志

9. warning mark　警告性标志

10. strong enough　足够坚固

11. solid and durable　坚固耐用

12. suited to the climate/transportation modes　适合气候条件/运输方式

13. number of packages　件数

14. package number　件号

15. pack sth. in...　某商品用……容器来装

16. pack... to...　把……装入……

17. pack sth. to... and... to...　把某商品装入……容器，再把若干个此种容器装入……

18. pack each... in... and... to...　每件……商品用……包装，若干件该商品装入……容器

19. Please mark the case with...　请在箱子上刷上……的标记。

20. withstand rough handling　经得起粗暴装卸

Chapter 7 Packing

Typical Sentences

1. Chinese chestnuts are packed in gunny bags.

2. Folding chairs are packed four pieces to a carton.

3. Please pack the vases a dozen to a wooden case and 100 to a FCL container.

4. Each T-shirt is packed in a polybag and 10 dozen to a box.

5. Please see to it that the packing is strong enough to withstand rough handling.

6. The export cartons lined with plastic sheets are proof against moisture and damage.

7. Please pack the goods according to our instructions.

8. The surface of each outer package should be marked "Fragile".

9. For the sake of safety, the cartons must be secured by metal bands.

10. Please take the necessary precautions so that the packing can protect the goods from rain or dampness in transit because these clothes are liable to be spoiled by water or moisture.

11. The fragile glassware needs special packing precautions against jolting.

12. The cases of the goods are to be marked with the initials of our company in a diamond as usual.

13. The packing of this shipment is shockproof and waterproof. Nevertheless we still marked the cartons with caution words like "Fragile", "Use No Hook" and "Do Not Drop".

14. Can you improve your inner packing? This is our design of the packing for your reference, which would probably help encourage sales.

15. To repack the goods in your required assortment will entail an additional packing charge of around US$2000.

16. Solid and durable, our cartons proved to be suitable packing for long distance transportation.

17. I'm afraid the cardboard boxes are not strong enough for such a heavy load.

18. By the way, we would like to know if neutral packing is acceptable.

19. The outer packing should be strong enough for transportation. As to inner packing, it must be attractive and helpful to the sales.

20. The extra packing charges should be borne by you.

Part V. Project Training

Project 1

Training Situation:

Mr. Smith, an importer from Hong Kong, has ordered a total amount of US$ 2000 of bamboo ware, including bamboo cases, baskets, bird cages, stools, chairs from China National

Import & Export Corporation, Shanghai Branch on FOB basis. They have agreed on price and terms of payment. Now they want to discuss about the packing of the articles.

Training Requirements:

The students are required to write a letter from the importer to the exporter giving instructions on packing and shipping marks.

Project 2

Training Situation:

You work for Peg Linda, Marketing Manager, at the headquarter of Shirly Textile Group. Your company will purchase 1000 dozen cotton stockings from the Second Textile Corporation of Shanghai.

Training Requirements:

The students are required to write a letter from the importer to the exporter for the term of packing and marking. Invent some details if necessary.

Part VI. Optional Study

I. Related Information

1. Packing containers include:

- Bag: May be made of strong paper, linen, canvas, rubber, etc.
- Sack: A large bag usually made of jute.
- Carton: Made of light but strong cardboard, or fiberboard with doubled lids and bottoms, fixed by glue, adhesive tapes, metal bands or wire staples. Sometimes a bundle of several cartons is made up into one package, held by metal bands.
- Case: A strong container made of wood. For extra strength it may have "battens". Sometimes thinner wood may be used with metal bands or wires passed around the case. The inside of the case may be "lined" with various material, damp resisting, tin foil, etc., to prevent damage by water, air or insects.
- Box: A small case, which may be of wood, cardboard or metal, and may have a folding (hinged) lid.
- Crate: This is a case, but one not fully enclosed. It has a bottom and a frame, sometimes open at the top. Crates are often built for the particular thing they have to carry.

- Cautious: Machinery packed in crates needs a special bottom (a skid) to facilitate handling.
- Drum: A cylinder-shaped container for carrying liquids, chemicals, paint, etc. It is usually made of metal. Certain dry chemicals (non-inflammable) or powders, are sometimes packed in wood or cardboard drums.
- Bale: A package of soft goods (e.g., cotton, wool, sheepskin) tightly pressed together and wrapped in a protective material. Usual size is 30*15*15 cm. It may be strengthened by metal bands.
- Can (or Tin): A small metal container in which small quantities of paint, oil or certain foodstuffs are packed.
- Carboy: A large glass container protected in a metal or wicker cage with soft packing between glass and cage. It is used for chemicals.
- Bundle: Miscellaneous goods packed without a container. A number of small cartons, etc., fixed together could be called a bundle.
- Container: A very large metal box for transport of goods by road, rail, sea or air. The advantage of packing goods in a container is easy to lift or move it during transport, and thus time is saved.
- Pallet: A large tray or platform for moving loads (by means of slings, etc), e.g., from a lorry into a train or onto a ship, and so save time for handling of separate items.

2. Some Expressions about Packing Marks

triangle 三角形		circle 圆形	
rectangle 长方形		hexagon 正六角形	
cross 十字形		downward triangle 倒三角形	
star 星形		square 正方形	
heart 心形		oval 椭圆形	
three diamond 三菱形		This side (end) up 此端/面向上	
Keep upright 竖立安放		Handle with care 小心轻放	
With care 小心搬运		Glass with care 小心玻璃	
No hook (Use no hook) 请勿用钩		Keep cool (keep in cool place) 放置冷处	
Keep dry 保持干燥		Keep away from boiler 远离锅炉	
Store away from boiler 远离锅炉		Keep away from heat 远离热源，隔离热气	
Guard against damp (wet) 勿使受潮		Keep flat (stow level) 注意平放	

Inflammable　易燃货物　　　　　Fragile　当心破碎

Fusible　易熔　　　　　　　　　Explosives　易爆货物

Poison　小心有毒　　　　　　　Perishable　易坏货物

II. Supplementary Specimen Letters

Specimen Letter 1　Reply to an Inquiry Regarding Packing

Dear Sirs,

　　Thank you for your inquiry of 20th November regarding our container service.

　　The shipping containers we provide are of two sizes, namely 20ft. and 40ft. They can be opened at both ends, thus making it possible to load and unload at the same time. For carrying goods liable to be spoiled by damp or water they have the advantage of being both water-tight and air-tight. Containers can be loaded and locked at the factory, if necessary, rendering pilferage impossible.

　　When separate consignments are carried in one container, if their ports of destination are the same, there will be a saving on freight charges, and an additional saving on insurance because of the lower premium charges for container-shipped goods.

　　We enclose a copy of our tariff and look forward to receiving your instructions.

　　　　　　　　　　　　　　　　　　　　　　　　　　　　Yours faithfully,

　　　　　　　　　　　　　　　　　　　　　　　　　　　　　(signature)

Notes

1. liable　*adj*. 易于……的，有……倾向的（后接介词 to），有责任的（后接介词 for）

　　She's liable to airsickness.　她容易晕机。

　　We are not liable for the delay in shipment.　我们对装运上的延误没有责任。

2. water-tight　不透水的，防水的

　　air-tight　不透气的，密封的

3. tariff　*n*. 关税，关税率，运费费率表

　　tariff barrier　关税壁垒

Specimen Letter 2　Seller's Proposal of Carton Packing

Dear Sirs,

　　We are pleased to inform you that starting with the next shipment we will use cartons instead of wooden cases to pack the shirts.

Chapter 7　Packing

> The benefits of such a change are as follows: (1) It will prevent skillful pilferage because the trace of pilferage will be more in evidence; (2) A carton lined with plastic sheets can protect shirts from moisture better than a wooden case; (3) Cartons are comparatively light and compact, and therefore are more convenient to handle.
>
> Our proposal above is based on the negative experiences of the past shipments where wooden cases have been used. We make this decision deliberately and look forward to your confirmation.
>
> Yours faithfully,
(signature)

Notes

1. "carton"指"纸板箱"，是海运中最常用的货物外包装的容器之一。其他常用的容器还有 wooden case(木箱)，olybag/plastic bag(塑料袋)，gunny sack(麻袋)，barrel(桶)，pallet(货盘)，container(集装箱)等。

2. skillful pilferage　擅偷者实施的偷窃

3. "because the trace of pilferage will be more in evidence"意为"因为偷窃的痕迹会更明显"。之所以把这一点作为更换包装的好处，是因为如果买卖方事先已在保险公司投保了"偷窃及提货不着险(Theft, Pilferage and Non-Delivery，简称 TPND)"，万一货物在运输途中被盗，就可在提货当天算起十天内向保险公司提出索赔。而保险公司首先要做的是检验现场及货物，看偷窃是否真的发生了。作为偷窃留下的痕迹，纸板箱被撕开的视觉效果比木箱被撬开的视觉效果更强烈，更容易给保险公司留下深刻印象，从而增大买卖方得到索赔的可能。

4. a carton lined with plastic sheets　内衬塑料层的纸板箱

5. "from moisture"指"防止潮湿"。"from"可用"against"代替，"moisture"可用"damp"代替。

6. Our proposal above is based on the negative experiences of the past shipments where wooden cases hare been used.

   "negative experiences"指"不好的经历"。根据上下文可推知，这些经历是指在过去使用木箱子装货的运输过程中发生的防潮效果差、装卸不便，或是发生盗窃时不利于举证索赔等情形。

   从语法角度看，"where"充当关系代词引导定语从句来修饰"experiences"一词；从表达效果看，这样处理能更紧凑地表达位于"where"一词前后的两层意思。

Specimen Letter 3   Seller Offering the Ideas of Packing and Shipping Marks

Dear Sirs,

　　Thank you for the letter of last week confirming most details of the sales contract we drafted while asking us to offer more information in the packing clause. We would like to specify the clause as follows.

　　The garments under the sales contract are packed in plastic bags, 5 dozen to a carton, 20 cartons to a pallet, 10 pallets to a FCL container. On the outside of each carton, ABC, the initials of your company in a diamond is stenciled as the shipping mark.

　　Please let us know your feedback on the above mentioned contents to be added to the packing clause of the sales contract.

Yours faithfully,
(signature)

Notes

1. packing clause （销售合同中的）包装条款
2. FCL   即 Full Container Load，整集装箱
3. feedback   相当于"responses"或"responding ideas".

Part VII. Exercises

I. Translate the following terms and expressions:

A. Into Chinese:

1. cardboard carton 　　　　　　2. in perfect condition
3. seaworthy packing 　　　　　　4. foamed plastics
5. fragile products 　　　　　　　6. kraft paper bag
7. shipping instructions 　　　　　8. in bad condition
9. in transit 　　　　　　　　　　10. double gunny bag

B. Into English:

1. 内包装 　　　　　　　　　　　2. 木箱
3. 装箱单 　　　　　　　　　　　4. 海洋运输
5. 外包装 　　　　　　　　　　　6. 容积
7. 出口包装 　　　　　　　　　　8. 中性包装
9. 粗鲁搬运 　　　　　　　　　　10. 包装要求

Chapter 7 Packing

II. Choose the best answer to complete each of the following sentences:

1. Upon arrival of the goods at the port of destination, we found that nearly 20% of the ____ had been broken, obviously attributed to improper ____.
   A. packages, packing   B. packet, packages
   C. packing, packages   D. package, packing

2. We suggest that this material ____ packed ____ tins of 600 grams, 20 tins ____ one wooden case.
   A. be, in, to   B. is, in, in
   C. in, with, in   D. be, with, in

3. Usually shipping marks should be stenciled on _____ packing.
   A. inner   B. outer   C. neutral   D. seaworthy

4. The buyer suggested that the packing of this article ____ improved.
   A. was to be   B. would be   C. had to be   D. be

5. We have made ____ clear that the goods should be packed in cartons.
   A. it   B. them   C. this   D. which

6. Our cotton T-shirts are packed ___ boxes ___ one dozen each, 200 boxes ____ a carton.
   A. with, in, to   B. with, to, in
   C. in, of, to   D. in, to, in

7. Women's leather gloves are packed ____ cartons ____ 100 pairs each.
   A. to, for   B. of, for   C. in, of   D. with, of

8. As requested, we will have the goods ____ in wooden cases, but you have to bear the extra ____ charges.
   A. packing, repacked   B. repacked, packing
   C. packing, packing   D. package, repacked

9. We sincerely hope the goods under your Order No.123 will reach you ____.
   A. in good conditions   B. in the good conditions
   C. in a good condition   D. in good condition

10. ____ is advisable for you to strengthen the case with double straps.
    A. It   B. This   C. That   D. The

III. Supply the missing words in the blanks of the following letter. The first letters are given:

Dear Sirs,
　　We (1)r_____ to our order No.12 for TV sets, which you are going to use cardboard (2)b_____ to pack.

We are afraid that cardboard boxes are not (3)s_____ enough for transportation by (4)s_____ so we propose that the consignment be sent by (5)c_____ service. What's more, soft packing stuffing material should be used all (6)a_____ the machines, not just under and over. This kind of packing does not (7)c_____ more, and it can effectively (8)p_____ the goods from being damaged by (9)r_____ handling. We believe these precautions are necessarily taken into (10)a_____.

We hope to receive your letter of confirmation soon.

Yours faithfully,

(signature)

IV. Translate the following sentences into English:

1. 瓷器易碎，因此我们务请你方注意包装。

2. 请注意我方 123 号订单项下的 1000 套茶具应装在垫有泡沫塑料的纸盒中。

3. 货物须经长途海洋运输，因此我们要求适合海运的包装。

4. 我们指明货物应装在木箱中并包装得足够坚固，以经得起码头上的粗鲁搬运。

5. 我们要求内包装小巧而精美以有助于销售，外包装轻便而坚固以易于搬运。

6. 青岛啤酒 300 毫升一瓶，10 瓶装一纸盒，2 盒装一纸箱。

7. 我们的咖啡用具要每套装一纸盒中，纸盒应设计精美，足以吸引最挑剔（selective）的买主。

8. 绿茶 100 克装一听，50 听装一纸箱，2 纸箱装一板条箱。

9. 我们希望货物抵达时完好并令你方完全满意。

10. 因水晶花瓶是贵重物品，请严格按照我方指令包装以免运输途中受损。

V. Translate the following letter into English:

敬启者：

感谢你方 6 月 1 日关于苹果酒的报价。我们高兴地订购 10000 瓶。请注意我方包装要求如下：

10000 瓶苹果酒，每瓶先套一塑料袋，再装入一较厚的精美的纸盒内，10 盒装入一垫有泡沫塑料的纸板箱中。纸箱应足够坚固，以经得起粗鲁搬运和长途运输。

请严格按照我方要求包装，以免运输途中受损。因圣诞节即将来临，务请尽早装运，以赶上旺销季节。

此致

VI. Write an English letter based on the following information:

1. 向卖方订购 10000 箱矿泉水。

2. 包装要求：每瓶 500 毫升，12 瓶装一纸箱，2 纸箱装一塑料箱，内包装务请美观以利销售，外包装务请坚固以便长途海运。

请卖方按要求包装并按时装运。

Chapter 8

Shipment

Chapter 8 Shipment

Task 1 Giving Shipping Instructions

Part I. Introduction

Shipment is one of the essential links in the chain of international trade. Goods can be transported by road, rail or air, but in most cases of international trade, by sea. The main activities of shipment include customs clearance, vessel chartering or shipping space booking, making out relative shipping documents and sending shipping advice.

Shipping instruction is a kind of document given by the buyer to the seller before the shipment for the requirement and instruction of the goods about its mode of packing, the stencil of the shipping mark and mode of transportation and so on.

Part II. Writing Skills

装船须知信函的结构如下：

1. 通知卖方信用证已开出，请求对方收到后尽快发货。(informing the seller that L/C has been opened and asking the seller to effect shipment without delay after receipt of it)

2. 指示卖方由什么公司/船运送货物或包装等。(instructing the seller by which shipping company/steamer to ship the goods or packing of the goods)

3. 希望货物令人满意并表示继续合作的愿望。(wishing the goods to be satisfactory and expressing the chance of business in the future)

4. 希望卖方早日发货/早日收到装运通知。(hoping the seller to ship the goods and to receive the shipping advice early)

Part III. Sample Letters

Sample 1 Giving Shipping Instructions

Dear Sirs,

We are in receipt of your telegram of May 6, from which we understand that you have booked our order for 2000 dozen shirts.

In reply, we have the pleasure of informing you that the confirmed, irrevocable Letter of Credit No.256, amounting to 15,000 has been opened this morning through the Shanghai Communication Bank. Upon receipt of the same, please arrange shipment of the goods booked by us with the least possible delay.

We are informed that S.S. Victoria is scheduled to sail from your city to our port on May 19. We wish that the shipment will be carried by that steamer.

Should this trial order prove satisfactory to our customer, we can assure you that repeat orders in increased quantities will be placed.

Your close cooperation in this respect will be highly appreciated. In the meantime we look forward to your shipping advice.

Yours sincerely,
(signature)

Notes

1. be in receipt of　已经收到
2. book our order　接受我方订单
3. amount to　总计，合计为，等于
4. be scheduled to　预计，预期
5. shipping advice　装运通知

Sample 2　Shipping Instructions

Dear Sirs,

We have received your fax of May 8th and noted that you have booked our Order No.251 for 8 sets of Model 230 machine. Our confirmation of the order will be forwarded to you in a few days.

It is of great importance to our buyers that the arrival date of this order should be arranged ASAP to meet their requirements. So you are supposed to ship the goods by a steamer of ABC Co. The main reason is that their steamers offer the shortest time for the journey between China and Germany. We shall appreciate it if you will endeavor to ship the consignments as follows:

Order No. 251: by S.S. "Victory" due to sail from Hamburg on 24 / 06 / 2004 arriving in Xiamen on 12 / 07 / 2004 respectively.

Thank you in advance for your cooperation.

Yours faithfully,
(signature)

Chapter 8 Shipment

Notes

1. endeavour *vi.& n.* 尽力，努力，力图

    make one's best endeavour(s)   尽最大努力

2. due   *adj.* （车、船）预定应到的，预期的，约定的

    e.g. The ship is due to leave (arrive) on or about May 10.

    该轮预计 5 月 10 号（或左右）离港/抵港。

3. ASAP   尽快，尽早，等同于 as soon as possible

4. respectively   *adv.* 分别地

Task 2   Urging a Timely Shipment

Part I. Introduction

Shipping is very important in foreign trade because goods sold by the seller have to be delivered to the buyer abroad, and the delivery of goods is made possible by (or transport) services. The business of foreign trade shipping is complicated. Therefore, a fairly good knowledge of the details regarding the procedures of shipment and the shipping documents is needed to fulfill a transaction and effect shipment in a safe, accurate and economical way.

In most movements of goods, there are usually three parties: the consignor, the consignee and the carrier. To ensure prompt delivery of the goods, consignors, carriers and consignees should keep in frequent contact with each other.

Part II. Writing Skills

When writing a letter about urging for shipment, you should pay attention to the following points:

1. Reference documents including their number and date.

2. Ask for their attention to the time limit and the consequence of the delay.

3. Requirement for the shipment in time.

4. Thanks for their cooperation.

Part III. Sample Letters

Sample 1   Buyer Urging Punctual Shipment

Dear Sirs,

We are now eager to know about the shipment of the racing bicycles as there has not

been any news about it from you since the L/C No.369 was issued two months ago.

By this letter, we wish to call your attention to the fact that the L/C will expire at the end of next week and that we are not going to extend it. This is due to the fact that the distributors and retailers at our end are in urgent need of the goods and we cannot afford to wait any longer. Therefore we will have to resort to other sources of bicycle suppliers if you fail to make the shipment in the time of validity.

We believe that all parties involved would definitely benefit from your prompt action of the shipment. We are looking forward to receiving your prompt shipping advice.

Yours faithfully,

(signature)

Notes

1. "since"后的时间状语从句用一般过去时，配合主句"there has not been"的现在完成时时态。

2. "call your attention to the fact that"意思是"以下情况请你们注意"。这种表达法展现了典型的商务英语风格，行文中起到委婉强调的作用。

3. "expire"即"to come to an end"，指"过期"。信用证上通常会规定有效期，超过这个期限，卖方（出口方）即使准确无误地备齐所有单证去银行申请议付，也是会被拒绝的。

4. "cannot afford to wait any longer"意思是"再也等不起了"。之所以这样讲，是因为此句中提到，在写信者（即进口商）本国等着供货的分销商和零售商们非常迫切地想要这批货。所以不能再允许延长信用证、再等下去了。

5. resort to 向……求助

    e.g. It is better that you resort to yourself than to others. 求人不如求己。

6. "in the time of validity"意思是"在（信用证）有效期内"。也可以这样表达：in the valid period，或者这样简洁地表达：within L/C validity。

Sample 2 Pressing for Prompt Shipment

Dear Sirs,

We wonder what has happened to our Order No.987 as nothing has been received from you about its shipment.

We stated explicitly at the time of placing the order the importance of punctual shipment

Chapter 8 Shipment

> as we had promised our customers that the goods could be supplied by the end of October. As a matter of fact, we have been urging you to execute the order in the past few weeks.
>
> Your delay in shipping our order has placed us in an awkward position. We must ask you to see your way clear to dispatch the goods in question as soon as possible so that we can assure our customers who may cancel their orders of the responsible time of delivery.
>
> Yours faithfully,
(signature)

Notes

1. punctual shipment   准时装运
2. execute the order   执行订单，履行订单
3. place us in an awkward position   使我们处于困境/尴尬境地
4. see your way clear to do sth.   设法做某事
5. in question   考虑之中的；被谈论着的，讨论中的，谈及的；争论中的
6. assure of   向……保证，使……确信，对……放心

Task 3   Giving Shipping Advice

Part I. Introduction

The sellers usually send a notice to the buyers immediately after the goods are loaded on board the ship, advising them of the shipment so that the buyers can make preparation for receiving the goods. Such a notice is known as Shipping Advice, which may include the following: S/C and L/C numbers, name of commodity, number of packages, total quantity shipped, name of vessel and its sailing date and sometimes even the total value of the goods.

Part II. Writing Skills

装运通知信函的结构如下：

1．通知买方合同项下的货物已于某日由某船运出。(informing the buyer that the goods under ×× contract has been shipped by S/S ×× on ×× date)

2．告知买方装运单据已寄出。(advising the buyer that the shipping documents have been sent out)

3．希望货物平安到达。(wishing the goods to arrive in good condition)

4. 感谢买方订货并希望再次收到对方的订单。(thanking the buyer for their order and wishing to receive their repeat orders)

Part III. Sample Letters

Sample 1   Shipping Advice

Dear Sirs,

　　We are pleased to inform you that the sewing machines you ordered on July 3 this year (Contract No.528) have now been shipped by S.S. Victoria sailing tomorrow from Shanghai to Liverpool.

　　Enclosed please find one set of the shipping documents covering this consignment as follows:

　　One copy of non-negotiable bill of lading

　　Commercial Invoice in duplicate

　　One copy of packing list

　　One copy of survey report

　　One copy of insurance policy

　　We hope this shipment will reach you in time and turn out to your entire satisfactions

　　　　　　　　　　　　　　　　　　　　　　Yours faithfully,

　　　　　　　　　　　　　　　　　　　　　　　　(signature)

Notes

1. Enclosed please find…　随函奉上，请查收

2. non-negotiable bill of lading　不可流通/转让的提单

3. commercial invoice　商业发票

4. packing list　装箱单

5. survey report　检验报告

6. turn out　证实，发觉是

Sample 2   Sending Out Shipping Advice

Dear Sirs,

　　Re: 35 Metric Tons of Groundnuts

　　We are glad to inform you that the subject goods have been shipped on board S/S Flying Cloud which is scheduled to leave here on or about March 26.

To facilitate your taking delivery of the goods on arrival, we have negotiated our sight draft under L/C No.356 with the following shipping documents through the Bank of China, Shanghai Branch:

Commercial Invoice in duplicate

One copy of non-negotiable Bill of Lading

Insurance Policy in duplicate

One copy of Certificate of Origin

One copy of Packing List

We hope the consignment will reach you in good order and look forward to further expansion of our business.

Yours truly,

(signature)

Notes

1. on board 在船（或车、飞机上）
2. non-negotiable 不可转让的
3. certificate of origin 原产地证书
4. consignment n. 一批（运送的）货物；寄售；寄售的货物
5. in good order 状况良好

Task 4   Asking for an Amendment to Shipment Clause

Part I. Introduction

The shipping clause is an important part of a contract signed between buyers and sellers. It involves the time of shipment, the port of loading and destination, the shipping documents, etc.

In foreign trade, it is the seller who designates the port of loading for the convenience of shipping the goods, while the port of destination is usually designated by the buyer. In most cases, one port of destination is specified.

In case of an export business covering a large amount of goods it is necessary to make shipment in several lots by several carriers sailing on different dates. When there are no or few ships sailing direct to the port of destination at the time or the amount of cargo for a certain port of destination is so small that no ships would like to call at the port, transshipment is necessary. Of course, partial shipment and transshipment should be allowed by the buyer in advance.

Also, as soon as goods are loaded on board a ship, the shipping company should issue a bill of lading to the shipper. The Bill of Lading, or the Ocean Bill of Lading, or B/L for short, is the document that the carrier, i.e., the shipping company makes, signs and issues to the consignor/exporter after receiving the cargo entrusted by the latter. It is a cargo receipt, an evidence of the carriage contract and most importantly, the document of ownership to the goods. Under the payment method of L/C, B/L is always one of the key documents that the beneficiary/exporter needs to submit when he/she asks for negotiation in the negotiation bank. The bill of lading together with the insurance policy and commercial invoices constitutes the chief shipping documents.

Part II. Writing Skills

When writing a letter about amending the shipment clause, you should pay attention to the following points:

1. Reference documents including their number and date.

2. The reason for amending the shipment clause.

3. State clearly how to make an amendment.

4. Thanks for their cooperation.

Part III. Sample Letters

Sample 1 Exporter Asking for Extension of L/C

Dear Sirs,

We are sorry to inform you that we have not been able to complete the shipment of the sports shoes under the order No.338 before November 31, which is the latest shipment date stipulated in the L/C.

As it had been reported by the media, the recent typhoon hit our city and damaged many buildings including several workshops of our factory, which caused one week's delay over the original deadline of completing the production of the shoes. If we had finished production one week earlier, the shipping company could have offered space and the consignment would have arrived at your end. However, the reality is that, from now on, the space of the route to your port will not be available until December 8, 2007. Therefore we would like to ask that you kindly extend the latest shipment date in the L/C.

Awaiting your favorable response.

Yours faithfully,

(signature)

Chapter 8 Shipment

Notes

1. hit   *v.*（风暴、疾病等）袭击，攻击

2. workshop   *n.* 车间，工作间

3. deadline   *n.* 最后期限，截止日期

4. If we had finished production one week earlier, the shipping company could have offered space and the consignment would have arrived at your end.

   此句可译为"要是我们提早一周完成生产的话，船运公司就会有舱位给我们，那么货物现在已到达贵方港口了。"这里作者用了虚拟语气来表达遗憾的心情。

5. favorable response   有利的回复，好的回复，佳音

Sample 2   Asking for Extension of L/C and Partial Shipment

Dear Sir or Madam,

   Re: 1500pcs of Cotton Shirting of Your Order No.113

   We regret very much to inform you that terrible typhoon struck our factory, which was badly damaged, making it impossible to ship the captioned goods in one lot.

   We faxed you, therefore, yesterday, asking you to allow us partial shipment, that is 500pcs. within the contracted time and the remainder in December. We hope you will agree to extend the credit till Jan.15. Though this is a case of Force Majeure, we are very sorry for it and we are doing everything in our power to recover our factory.

   We should be obliged if you could kindly understand the situation and you would comply with our request.

                                                                    Yours faithfully,

                                                                    (signature)

Notes

1. struck   *vt.* strike 的过去式，侵袭，打，撞击，冲击，罢工，打动

2. remainder   *n.* 剩余物，余额

3. Force Majeure   不可抗力（an unexpected or uncontrollable event）

4. recover   *vt.* 恢复，补偿

Part IV. Useful Expressions and Typical Sentences

Useful Expressions

1. shipper/consignor   货主，委托人

2. shipping service 航运业

3. shipping company 船运公司

4. forwarding agent 运输代理行

5. shipping instruction 装运须知

6. shipping advice 装船通知

7. on board 已装船

8. optional port 选择港

9. partial shipment 分运

10. transshipment 转船

11. The steamer is scheduled to leave Guangzhou on...
    该货轮计划于……时驶离广州。

12. The consignment under contract No×× has been shipped via...
    ××号合同项下的货物已装上……起运。

13. As to the shipping documents, enclosed please find...
    至于运输单据，请看随信所附的……

14. We feel delighted to inform you that... 我们高兴地通知贵方……

15. One set of... have been sent to you. 一套……已寄给你们。

16. We take pleasure in telling you that we have completed the shipment of...
    我们很高兴地告知贵方，我们已完成了对……的装船。

17. We make sure that...will have our full attention.
    我们保证会尽心办理贵方的……

18. The delay in shipment will be detrimental to... 误了装运期将对……带来损害。

19. book shipping space on... for... 为……在……上订舱位

20. ... is few and far between. ……稀少。

Typical Sentences

1. We are glad to inform you that the goods you ordered have been well prepared and the shipment will be made upon the receipt of L/C.

2. As the latest shipment date stipulated in the L/C is October 31, 2007, please see to it that you make the shipment not later than the above date.

3. We take pleasure in telling you that the shipment of the shirts originally scheduled to be made in December can be advanced to October as the result of the efforts by all parties involved.

Chapter 8　Shipment

4. Owing to the delay of the scheduled steamer we have failed to effect the shipment within the L/C validity. Would you please extend the shipping period of the L/C for one more month?

5. It must be reiterated that prompt shipment is one of the essential requirements to obtain our orders.

6. We are sending you one set of clean on board bill of lading through the bank.

7. Enclosed please find the copies of B/L, commercial invoices and the insurance policy.

8. We regret to inform you that we cannot advance the shipment as you requested as we have been told by the shipping company that there will be no space available before the end of next month.

9. We would like to try to advance the shipment as you wish but cannot guarantee to absolutely make it.

10. Would you please cable the shipping advice as soon as possible as there is still no news about the shipment from you and the L/C is due to expire next week.

11. Please expedite the shipment trying your best.

12. We shall cable you in due course the name of the chartered steamer and its estimated arrival time.

13. The Chinese art crafts you ordered have been shipped already and your future order will continue to receive our prompt attention.

14. We should be glad if you could manage to ship the goods by S.S. "East Wind" sailing from July 1.

15. We shall appreciate it if you effect shipment as soon as possible, thus enabling our buyers to catch the brisk demand at the start of the season.

16. Owing to the delay in opening the relative L/C, shipment cannot be made as contracted and should be postponed to the end of next month.

17. Please amend the covering Letter of Credit to allow partial shipment, under advice to us.

18. As the only direct steamer, which calls at our port once a month, has just departed, the goods can only be shipped next month.

19. You will please do your very best to hasten shipment. We hope that by the time you receive the letter, you will have the goods ready for shipment.

20. We wish to advice you that the goods under S/C No.GZ-001 went forward per S.S. "Dongfeng" on June 4, to be transshipped in Hong Kong and are expected to reach your port in July.

Part V. Project Training

Project 1

Training Situation:

You are the Administrative Assistant to Mrs Hannah Mbora, Sales and Marketing Manager of the Lualaba Tree and Plant Supply Company, Cabinda Road, Kinshasa, Zaire. The company sells trees to customers throughout the world.

Training Requirements:

Write a letter to one of your customers informing him the arrangements you have made for the transport of 200 pine trees Art. No.246. Invent some details if necessary.

Project 2

Training Situation:

From: Acme Products, 4562 West Rose St, Newtown, CA, 99996, USA

To: East China Export Company, 3543 West Tower, Shanghai, 11118, China

Re: Order No.A-452

Training Requirements:

You are required to write a letter to ask the company to change the shipping destination from San Francisco to Los Angeles, the shipping date and vessel from November 15 on S.S. *Spring Breeze* to November 18 on S.S. *Windrunner*.

Part VI. Optional Study

I. Related Information

Freight may travel by rail, plane, ship, truck, or even pipeline.

The greatest advantage of railroad freight is its low cost for shipping heavy and bulky commodities. Shipments much too heavy for the parcel post weight limits and too expensive to send by express may be sent by railroad freight. Lumber, coal, iron ore, and chemicals are a few items particularly suited to this type of transportation.

Today trucks carry an increasing amount of goods. This method of shipping is very profitable for short hauls (短途运输). Even on longer runs it has the advantage of picking up and delivering small or large shipments anywhere as business demands. Trucks are not limited to fixed schedules as the railroads and airlines.

Chapter 8 Shipment

Trucking companies often work together with the railroads in moving goods even though they are competitors. Goods may be loaded in the trailer at a business; then the trailer is driven to the railroad station and loaded on a flatcar that will transport it to its destination. When it arrives at its destination, the trailer is unloaded, hitched up to a truck, an moved to the consignee's business.

Many freight shipments are made by water, which is a slower but less expensive means of freight transportation. Commodities such as coal, grain, chemicals, and iron ore are most often shipped by this means.

Air freight service is more expensive than land or water transportation. However, other factors besides cost must be considered in choosing a shipping method. For example, in a shipment of replacement machine parts vitally needed by a certain day, time is much more important than the shipping cost. Food and other perishable goods might also be shipped by air freight.

Pipelines are an important means of transporting types of commodities. This form of service is being used for transporting crude oil to refineries far away from the oil wells. It is also being used for supplying natural gas to consumers and industrial users some distance away from the source of supply.

II. Supplementary Specimen Letter

Specimen Letter 1   Transshipment

Dear Sirs,

As required in your letter of March 9, we are pleased to provide the following information for your reference:

1. There are about 2 to 3 sailings weekly from Shanghai to Hong Kong.

2. Arrangements have been made with the ABC Line, which has one sailing approximately on the 10th every month from Hong Kong to West African ports. Shipping space is to be booked through their Shanghai Agents, who communicate with the line by fax. After receipt of the Line's reply accepting the booking, their Shanghai Agents will issue a Through Bill of Lading. Therefore, with the exception of unusual condition which may happen accidentally, the goods will be transshipped from Hong Kong without delay.

3. In general the freight for transshipment from Hong Kong is higher than that from the U.K. or continental port, but ABC Line agrees to the same freight, the detailed rates of which are shown on the 2 appendices to this letter.

If you want to have the goods transshipped at Hong Kong, your L/C must reach us well before the shipment month so as to enable us to book space with the Line's Agents.

We assure you of our best attention at all times.

Yours sincerely,

(signature)

Notes

1. transshipment   转船

2. sailing   *n.* 船运

   e.g. There are no more sailings this month.

   本月不再有船。

3. ABC Line   ABC 航运公司

4. Through Bill of Lading   联运提单

5. with the exception of   除……之外

6. appendix (appendices)   *n.* 附件，附录

Specimen Letter 2   Confirming Shipment

Dear Sirs,

Order No.365 for Silk Blouses

We wish to confirm our cable of today, which reads as follow:

"ORDER 365 SILK BLOUSES 2000 DOZEN SHIPPED SS CROWN 11/6".

The above cable is self-explanatory.

We now have much pleasure in sending you herewith our invoice covering the above shipment which went forward on S.S. Crown against your order No.365 of 15th April. We trust the goods will reach you in due course and give you entire satisfaction, the quality being equal to, if not better than, that of former shipments. As desired, we have drawn upon you for the net amount of $15000 at sight through the Italian Commercial Bank and would ask you to give our draft your kind protection as usual.

We hope to receive your repeat orders but wish to inform you that, owing to the advance in the cost of silk, we shall very probably be compelled to raise our prices in the immediate future to the silk blouses.

We await your reply.

Yours sincerely,

(signature)

Chapter 8 Shipment

Notes

1. self-explanatory   自明的，不需要加以说明的

2. have (much) pleasure in doing sth   很高兴做某事

3. be equal to   等同于

4. as desired   即 as requested，按照请求

5. draw upon sb   即 draw on sb，向某人开立汇票

6. in the immediate future   在不久的将来

Part VII. Exercises

I. Translate the following terms and expressions:

A. Into Chinese:

1. shipping company
2. port of shipment
3. shipping documents
4. port of destination
5. liner
6. port of loading
7. tramp
8. port of discharge/unloading
9. sailing date
10. transshipment

B. Into English:

1. 运输方式
2. 装运通知
3. 装运时间
4. 装运要求
5. 原产地证明书
6. 舱位
7. 分批装运
8. 大宗商品，散装货
9. 运输标志，唛头
10. 运输代理，货代

II. Choose the best answer to complete each of the following sentences:

1. We find ____ transshipment and partial shipment of the printed shirting are not allowed.

   A. that   B. what   C. where   D. there

2. We have received your letter of the 1st March ____ us to effect shipment as soon as possible.

   A. to ask   B. that ask   C. asking   D. for asking

3. I am sorry that I am not ____ a position to promise you to do business on your terms.

   A. at   B. in   C. on   D. for

4. The shipment ____ Contract No.333 has arrived here duly (及时地).
   A. under	B. by	C. for	D. in

5. The additional charges are ____ your own account.
   A. for	B. at	C. of	D. on

6. The goods ____ question are all best sellers for their superior quality.
   A. in	B. out of	C. at	D. on

7. Direct steamers to your port are few ____ the summer season.
   A. at	B. for	C. with	D. during

8. The goods will be shipped ____ October 9.
   A. in	B. to	C. on	D. with

9. Please try your best to ship our order ____ that steamer.
   A. by	B. for	C. in	D. with

10. Please note that Item No.789 can be certainly promised for immediate shipment ____ receipt of your order.
    A. if	B. whether	C. upon	D. at

III. Supply the missing words in the blanks of the following letter. The first letters are given:

Dear Sirs,

In (1)r_____ to your letter urging the shipment we (2)r_____ being unable to ship the 10 containers of Chinese cotton toys by direct steamer.

The direct steamers are very rare from here to your (3)p_____ and the shipping space has been fully (4)b_____ up to the end of the month after next. Therefore we would suggest that you (5)p_____ us to ship via Hong Kong and such arrangement will result in the (6)p_____ arrival of the cargo.

We hope you can (7)u_____ that we are not the only exporter who has the difficulty in (8)o_____ shipping space.

We look forward to (9)r_____ your early confirmation on this (10)i_____.

Yours faithfully,

(signature)

IV. Translate the following sentences into English:

1. 我们可以保证 5 月 1 日以前装运。

2. 如果你方能修改地毯的报价，我们将向你方大量订购。

3. 我们希望货物分两批等量装运，每批 30000 台。

4. 很遗憾我们无法将装运期提前到 8 月初。

5. 现通知，9 月份没有开往你方港口的直达轮，需要在香港转船。

6. 你方最早什么时候可以装运？

7. 目前看我们最早能在 3 月份交货。不过我向你保证，如有可能，我们将尽最大努力提前交货。

8. 为了满足你方的迫切需求，我们希望允许分批装运。

9. 货物的一切运输费用应该由你方负担。

10. 对所有产品我们都规定了必须满足的最低质量要求。

V. Translate the following letter into English:

敬启者：

你方 4 月 5 日来信收到。

今歉告，尽管我方做了极大努力，仍未预订到直达雅加达（Jakarta）的轮船舱位。我方轮船公司告知，中国港口与雅加达之间暂无定期船只，因而我方很难将此 10000 公吨白糖直运雅加达。

鉴于我们所面临的困难，请允许在香港转船，因为香港很容易转运。贵方若能同意我方的要求并理解我方所处境况，当不胜感激。

谨启

VI. Write an English letter based on the following information:

收到客户 6 月 10 日关于第 65 号合同的来函。因 8 月 15 日前没有集装箱船，不能提前装船，深表遗憾。但可确保货物在合同规定时间内装船。

VII. 案例分析：

误解装运条款引起争端

某粮油进出口公司于 1994 年 4 月以 CIF 条件与英国乔治贸易有限公司成交一笔出售棉籽油贸易，总数量为 840 公吨，允许分批装运。对方开来信用证中有关装运条款规定："840M/Tons of cottonseed oil. Loading port: Guangzhou Partial shipments are allowed in tow lots. 460M/Tons to London not later than September 15, 1994. 380M/Tons to Liverpool not later than October 15, 1994."（840 公吨棉籽油。装运港：广州，允许分二批装运。460 公吨于

1994年9月15日前至伦敦，380公吨于1994年10月15日前到利物浦）。粮油进出口公司于8月3日在黄浦港装305公吨至伦敦，计划在月末再继续装至伦敦的余数155公吨，9月末装至利物浦的380公吨，第一批305公吨装完后即备单办理议付。但单据寄到国外后，开证行于8月15日提出单证有如下不符：

1. 我信用证只允许分二批（in two lots）装运，即460公吨至从伦敦，380公吨至利物浦。你于8月3日只装305公吨至伦敦，余下155公吨准备继续再装，这样违背了我信用证规定。

2. 我信用证规定装运港为广州港（Loading port: Guangzhou），根据你提单上记载，其装运港为黄浦（Huangpu），不符合我信用证要求。

如何通过所学函电知识解决此问题？

Chapter 9

Insurance

Task 1   Requesting the Exporter to Cover Insurance

Part I. Introduction

Insurance is one of the most important parts in international trade. Whatever mode of transport is adopted, there will be many risks to cargo transportation at any stage of the transit. So, exporters or importers need to cover insurance on their goods with insurance companies against different risks.

People originally used insurance to cover losses at sea, where risks were very great. Now it has become a vast subject, entering into almost every activity of human beings. Insurance is against risk. The idea of insurance is to obtain some indemnity in the event of any happenings that causes loss of money. It provides a pool or fund into which the many contribute and out of which the few who suffer loss are compensated.

Part II. Writing Skills

When asking the seller to cover insurance for the buyer, the following points should be mentioned:

- the exact business terms adopted
- the exact kind of insurance requested
- the sum of the premium

Part III. Sample Letters

Sample 1   Importer Asks Exporter to Cover Insurance

Dear Sirs,

Re: Our Order No.235 for 1,500 sets of Panda Color Television

We wish to refer you to our Order No.235 for 1,500 sets of Panda Color Television, from which you will see that this order is placed on a CFR basis.

In order to save time and simplify procedures, we now desire to have the shipment insured at your end. We shall be pleased if you will arrange to insure the goods on our behalf against All Risks for 110% of the full invoice value, i.e., US$120,000. May we suggest that you would follow our proposal.

We shall of course refund you the premium upon receipt of your debit note or, if you like, you may draw on us at sight for the amount required.

Chapter 9 Insurance

We sincerely hope that our request will meet with your approval.

Yours faithfully,

(signature)

Notes

1. cover insurance   投保，办保险；相当于 arrange insurance, effect insurance, take out insurance

2. refer you to our Order No.235   请你查看一下我方第 235 号订单

   refer sb. to sth.   请某人查看某物/事，使（某人）向……咨询

   e.g. They refer us to your company for information.

   他们让我们向贵公司咨询有关信息。

3. This order is placed on a CFR basis.

   这批货是按 CFR 订购的。（CFR 指运费在内价，成本加运费价。）

4. at your end   即 in your place /on your side，你处，你方

5. on our behalf   代表我方

6. for 110% of the full invoice value   按全部发票金额的 110%

7. May we suggest that you would follow our proposal?

   may   表示请求许可，是正式的讲法。

   follow   v. 遵循

8. refund you the premium   将保险费偿付给你方

9. debit note   索款通知

10. draw on us at sight for the amount required   开即期发票向我们收取所需金额

Sample 2   Requesting Exporter to Cover Insurance

Dear Sirs,

Re: Order No.435

With regard to our order of 1,500 men's jackets we have issued an irrevocable L/C at sight which takes your company as the beneficiary. You will be advised by Shanghai Branch of the Bank of China very soon. So you can prepare for production and shipment without any concern.

There is another issue we want to request here. As we know, the price that has been stipulated in both the S/C and L/C is based on CFR term and hence insurance lies within our

responsibilities. For the sake of convenience we wonder whether you could have the goods insured, on behalf of us, against WPA and TPND for 110% of the invoice value at your end. The premium charge is, of course, for our account.

　　Hope this request will meet with your approval.

Yours faithfully,
(signature)

Notes

1. "with regard to"指"关于"。表达该意思的词或短语很多，常用的有：regarding，referring to，as to，about，with reference to，in regard to 等。

2. "without any concern"意为"不用担心"。之所以这样讲，是因为信用证已开，有了银行的付款保证，只要出口人在有效期内交齐信用证要求的单证，并确保所交单证填写无误，就一定能收到货款。若信用证没开，就没有第三方（银行）的信用保证，出口方则存在收款风险。

3. "S/C"即"sales confirmation"（销售确认书）的英文简称，也有人认为是"sales contract"（销售合同）的简称。其实两者并无本质差别，都是买卖双方签订的书面销售协议。若都在其中对双方的某些商务行为作了法律后果的界定，就都可以作为日后用于遵循法律途径解决争议和纠纷的依据之一。

4. "insurance lies within our responsibilities"是外贸函电的较正式的说法，也可以说"We (The buyer) should have the goods insured."

5. "on behalf of us"是整个句子的状语，可以放在句末，但在这里把它像插入语般地放在这个位置是行文的自然节奏，说话人讲到这里时想强调这一点，就先讲了。英语母语人士在讲话或撰文时往往如此。

6. "WPA and TPND"指"水渍险和偷窃及提货不着险"。"WPA"全称"With Particular Average"，是三种基本险之一，比另一种基本险——平安险多保了由自然灾害造成的单独海损。"TPND"全称"Theft, Pilferage and Non-Delivery"，是一般附加险中的一种。

7. "for sb's account"即"paid by sb."

　　e.g. According to the prevailing practice, the extra premium of the additional insured value and insured coverage should be for the buyer's account.
　　按照目前的惯例，对额外的保险金额及保险险种所收的保险费应由买方支付。

Chapter 9　Insurance

Task 2　Type of Coverage Adopted

Part I. Introduction

The Coverage of Insurance

There are three basic types of coverage, namely, Free From Particular Average (FPA), With Particular Average (WA/WPA) and All Risks (AR), which are known as basic risks. Besides, there are two additional risks, General Additional Risks and Special Additional Risks. General Additional Risks include Theft, Pilferage & Non-Delivery Risks (TPND) (偷窃、提货不着险), Fresh and /or Rain Water Damage Risks (淡水雨淋险), Shortage Risk (短量险), Intermixture & Contamination Risks (混杂、玷污险), Leakage Risk (渗漏险), Clash & Breakage Risks (碰损、破碎险), Taint of Odor Risk (串味险), Sweating & Heating Risks (受潮受热险), Hook Damage Risk (钩损险), Rust Risk (锈损险), and Breakage of Packing Risk (包装破裂险). Special Additional Risks include Failure to Deliver Risk (交货不到险), Import Duty Risk (进口关税险), On Deck Risk (舱面货物险), Rejection Risk (拒收险), Aflatoxin Risk (黄曲霉素险), War Risk (战争险) and Strikes Risk (罢工险). Additional risks cannot be covered independently and should go with FPA, WPA, or All Risks.

Part II. Writing Skills

When adopting a certain type of coverage, the following points should be mentioned:
- the relevant goods and the documents No.
- informing the addressee the type of coverage adopted
- confirmation of the premium

Part III. Sample Letters

Sample 1　Informing Buyer of Insurance Information

Dear Sirs,

　　Re: CIF Insurance for Tape Recorders

In reply to your letter of August 8th in which you inquired about CIF Insurance for Tape Recorders that we mentioned to you on August 1st, we provide you with the information as follows.

　　As to the CIF deal, we usually cover insurance against All Risks with the People's Insurance Company of China as per the relevant Ocean Marine Cargo Clauses of the People's Insurance Company of China dated January 1st, 1981. If you claim ICC clauses for insurance, we would be very glad to satisfy your demand on condition that the margin of expenses will be paid by you.

If you like, we could also provide additional coverage for goods with the extra cost on your account. In such case, we will send you a receipt of cost issued by the relevant insurer. As usual, the amount insured is 110% of the invoice value. If you ask for higher percentage, we could arrange accordingly provided the extra cost is at your expense.

We hope the above-mentioned information is of interest to you and we are looking forward to receiving your order soon.

Yours faithfully,

(signature)

Notes

1. on condition that   如果……，在……条件下

2. margin   差额

3. provided *conj*. 以……为条件，假如

4. at your expense   由你方付费，由你方负担

Sample 2   Covering Insurance for the Buyer

Dear Sirs,

"Panda" Brand TV Sets

We are in receipt of your letter of July 15 asking us to cover insurance on the captioned goods for you.

In compliance with your request, we have contacted the insurance company here and covered the goods with them against All Risks and Clash & Breakage Risks for 130% of the invoice value, totaling US$16500. The policy is being prepared accordingly and will be forwarded to you by airmail within one week. Please pay the premium by check into our account with the Bank of China, Beijing Branch.

For your information, we are arranging shipment of the above goods by S.S. Victory sailing for your port on or about August 8 and hope they will reach you in due course.

Yours faithfully,

(signature)

Chapter 9 Insurance

Notes

1. the captioned goods   标题项下的货物
2. in compliance with   遵从，遵照；依从，按照
3. Clash & Breakage Risks   碰损破碎险
4. total   *v.* 总计为
5. in due course   及时地，在适当的时候

Task 3   Reply to the Letter Requesting Excessive Insurance

Part I. Introduction

It is general practice to have the goods covered for 110% of the invoice value, if the buyer wants to cover for more than 110%, then the extra premium will be for his account.

Insurance policy or certificate is an evidence of insurance issued by the insurer or underwriters to the insured. On the other hand, it's also a contract between the aforesaid parties, which stipulates each party's rights and responsibilities.

The terms of insurance in a contract usually contains the insurance to be covered by whom, against certain kinds of risks, for certain amount of money, and as per what kind of clause it is to be executed. Therefore, the following sentence pattern should be remembered.

to be covered by… against… for … as per…

The People's Insurance Company of China (PICC) established in 1949, is the sole state-owned insurance organization in China.

Part II. Writing Skills

When replying to the letter requesting excessive insurance, the following points should be mentioned:

- the relevant goods and the documents No.
- the extra premium agreed
- the party paying the extra premium

Part III. Sample Letters

Sample 1   Asking for Excessive Insurance

Dear Sirs,

   Thank you for your letter of March 21 informing us that the lathes we booked with you are now ready for shipment.

As contracted, insurance on the goods should be effected for 10% above the invoice value. But as you know the recent situation in the countries along the way from Shanghai to our port is very serious, we wonder if you could insure against War Risk in addition to the previously agreed FPA for 150% of the invoice value. If so, the extra premium will be for our account.

Your early confirmation of the above will be much appreciated.

Yours faithfully,

(signature)

Notes

1. lathe　　*n.* 车床
2. ready for shipment　　备妥待运
3. as contracted　　按照合同，照约定
4. War Risk　　战争险
5. for our account　　由我方负担（支付）

Sample 2　Reply to a Request for Excessive Insurance

Dear Sir or Madam,

We have received your fax concerning insurance of the goods under contract No.116.

As you know, we generally cover insurance against WPA in the absence of definite instructions from our clients for the invoice value plus 10%. If you desire to cover all risks, we can provide such coverage at a higher premium, and breakage is an additional risk, for which an extra premium will have to be charged. Claims are payable only for that part of the loss, that is over 5%.

But with a view to our long amicable business relationship, we decided to comply with you this time. But you should bear in mind that even if the additional risk of breakage has been insured, the cover is subject to 5% franchise. In other words, no claims for damage can be obtained, if the breakage is examined to be less than 5%. For your earlier attention, we have sent you an E-mail to that effect yesterday.

We trust the above information will serve your purpose and await your further news.

Yours faithfully,

(signature)

Chapter 9 Insurance

Notes

1. in the absence of 在……缺席（不在）时，缺少……时
2. cover   *n.* 保险

   v. 保险，投保。后可接所保的货物、投保的险别和被保险人。

   e.g. We shall cover the goods against all risks.

   We shall cover all risks and war risk for you.

   This insurance policy covers us against breakage.
3. amicable   *adj.* 友好的，和睦的

   to settle a question in an amicable way   用友好的方式解决问题
4. comply with   即 follow，按要求做，照做
5. franchise   保险契约规定的免赔限度，免赔额
6. to that effect   带有那个意思，大意是那样
7. serve your purpose   达到你方目的

Part IV. Useful Expressions and Typical Sentences

Useful Expressions

1. the insurer   承保人，保险人
2. underwriters   保险商
3. insurance company   保险公司
4. insurance agent   保险经纪
5. insurance policy   保险单
6. insurance value/amount   保险金额
7. insurance premium   保险费
8. insurance coverage   保险范围（可指险别和/或金额范围）
9. Free from Particular Average (FPA)   平安险
10. With Particular Average (WPA/WA)   水渍险
11. All Risks (AR)   一切险
12. General Additional Risk   一般附加险
13. Special Additional Risk   特殊附加险
14. War Risk   战争险
15. with a franchise of ××%   有一个××%的免赔率
16. cover/effect/arrange/take out/attend to/provide/handle insurance   投保，买保险
17. cover the goods against ... risk   为货物投保……险

173

18. insure ... with ... insurance company   向……保险公司投保……货物
19. for one's account   由……支付
20. the People's Insurance Company of China (PICC)   中国人民保险公司

Typical Sentences

1. We will insure the goods against WPA and TPND for the invoice value plus 10%.

2. Many export-oriented Chinese manufacturers choose to insure their consignment with the PICC.

3. We would like to take out insurance on your behalf.

4. Considering the port of destination is not far from the war zone we suggest you to cover the insurance for the shipment against All Risks and War Risk.

5. When we cover insurance for goods made of glass it is necessary that Risk of Clash & Breakage is included.

6. I'm calling to ask whether your insurance company allows the foodstuffs to be insured against the risk of deterioration.

7. As the exporter, we follow the prevalent practice that our CIF price covers the insurance against WPA and any extra premium of additional risks should be for the importer's account.

8. It has become the common sense that the insurance of goods traded on the basis of CFR or FOB term is supposed to be arranged by the buyer.

9. Unless otherwise regulated in the L/C, the negotiation bank will permit the beneficiary/exporter to deliver either of insurance policy, insurance certificate or open policy for negotiation.

10. To cover a special additional risk only costs a slightly higher premium.

11. FPA covers all total losses incurred by natural calamities and/or accidents, and partial losses by natural calamities.

12. We want to know your lowest rates FPA.

13. The premium of the cargo is at the rate of 1.5% of the goods value you declare to insure.

14. In the absence of specific instructions from our clients we usually cover insurance against WPA and War Risk.

15. The shipment has been insured as per warehouse-to-warehouse clause and subject to the Ocean Marine Cargo Clauses.

16. Insurance provides a pool or fund into which many contribute their money and from which the few suffering losses are compensated.

17. These leather shoes need to be insured against the Fresh Water &/or Rain Damage (FWRD) and the risk of Intermixture & Contamination in addition to WPA.

18. The policy holder must submit the claim within 30 days after the losses of the insured cargo are found.

19. The insurance company insures this risk with a 5% franchise.

20. We regret our inability to comply with the buyer's request for covering insurance for 150% of the invoice value, because our contract stipulated that insurance should be covered for 110% of the invoice value.

Part V. Project Training

Project 1

Training Situation:

You represent Sichuan Tea Company. Mr. Black, an American buyer has ordered 200 cases of black tea from you on a CIF basis. You are now negotiating with him about the insurance clauses.

Training Requirements:

Your letter will include:

- which insurance company to insure with
- what risks to cover
- the insurance amount

Project 2

Training Situation:

You, as an exporter of fertilizers, got a letter from your client. Your client asked you to arrange for insurance with the PICC for their Order No. 342 on their behalf and for their account. He promised to send the premium by T/T next week. He also asked you for advice on the risks to be covered.

Training Requirements:

The students are required to write a letter of reply according to the above situation.

Part VI. Optional Study

I. Related Information

Duties of the Seller as to Insurance

1. It is the duty of the seller to procure at his own cost from an underwriter or insurance company of good repute a policy of marine insurance, evidencing a valid and subsisting contract

which shall be available for the benefit of the buyer, covering the goods during the whole of the course of transit contemplated in the contract of sale, including customary transhipment, if any.

The seller shall not be bound to procure a policy covering war risks unless:

(1) special provision to this effect shall have been made in the contract of sale, or

(2) the seller shall have received prior to the shipment of the goods or their delivery into the custody of the carrier, as the case may be, notice from the buyer to procure a policy covering such risks.

Unless such special provision shall have been made in the contract of sale, any additional cost of procuring a policy covering war risks shall be borne by the buyer.

2. If the policy is not available when the documents are tendered, the seller can buy a Certificate of Insurance. A Certificate of Insurance is issued by an underwriter or insurance company of good repute. It reproduces the essential terms and conditions of the original policy for the goods mentioned in the bill(s) of lading and invoice(s). It is proof of marine insurance. The seller guarantees that he will, on the demand of the buyer, produce the policy referred to in the certificate.

3. Unless it is usual in that particular trade for the seller to tender to the buyer an Insurance Broker's Cover Note in lieu of a policy of insurance, such a Cover Note does not usually represent a policy of insurance.

The value of the goods for insurance purpose is fixed in accordance with the usage of the particular trade, but in the absence of any such usage it shall be the invoice CIF value of the goods to the buyer, less freight payable if any, on arrival, and plus a marginal profit of 10% of the said invoice CIF value, after deduction of the amount of freight, if any, payable on arrival.

Expressions about Insurance

risk of breakage　破碎险

risk of clashing　碰损险

risk of rust　生锈险

risk of hook damage　钩损险

risk of contamination (tainting)　污染险

insurance against total loss only (TLO)　全损险

risk of deterioration　变质险

risk of packing breakage　包装破裂险

risk of inherent vice　内在缺陷险

Chapter 9 Insurance

risk of normal loss (natural loss)　途耗或自然损耗险

risk of spontaneous combustion　自然险

risk of contingent import duty　进口关税险

insurance against war risk　战争险

Air Transportation Cargo War Risk　航空运输战争险

Overland Transportation Insurance War Risk　陆上运输战争险

insurance against strike, riot and civil commotion (SRCC)　罢工、暴动、民变险

insurance against extraneous risks, insurance against additional risks　附加险

risk of theft, pilferage and nondelivery (TRND)　盗窃提货不着险

risk of fresh and/of rain water damage(wetting)　淡水雨淋险

risk of leakage　渗漏险

risk of shortage in weight/quantity　短量险

risk of sweating and/or heating　受潮受热险

risk of bad odour (change of flavour)　恶味险，变味险

risk of mould　发霉险

on deck risk　舱面险

health insurance　疾病保险，健康保险

sickness insurance　疾病保险

insurance for medical care　医疗保险

major medical insurance　巨额医药费保险

insurance during a period of illness　疾病保险

life insurance　人寿保险

endowment insurance　养老保险

insurance on last survivor　长寿保险

II. Supplementary Specimen Letter

Specimen Letter 1　Covering Insurance for the Buyer

Dear Sirs,

　　We are glad to notify you that the shipment of 5000 cases of Pepsi Coke under contract No.236 will be effected per S.S. "East Wind" which is scheduled to sail for your port on May 5th.

　　Unless otherwise instructed, we will cover insurance for 110% of the invoice value against WPA as per CIC at our end. If you wish to secure protection against breakage, such insurance can be easily arranged upon payment of an extra premium, which will be on your account, but at a favorable rate, because we are on good terms with PICC. Through our long-term business experience with them, we find that the underwriter grants quite a handsome premium rebate at regular intervals.

Yours faithfully,
(signature)

Notes

1. sail for　启航，动身

2. unless otherwise instructed　除非另行规定

3. on your account　由你方支付，由你方负担

4. at a favorable rate　以较优惠的费率

5. be on good terms with　与……关系好，与……相处得好

6. premium rebate　保险费回扣

7. at regular intervals　每隔一定时间

Specimen Letter 2　Information about Insurance Rate

Dear Sirs,

We thank you for your order No.428 for 1,200 Giant Brand bicycles, which is placed on C & F basis.

In reply, we would like to inform you that most of our clients are placing their orders with us on CIF basis. This will save their time and simplify procedures. May we suggest that you would follow this practice.

For your information, we usually effect insurance with the People's Insurance Company of China for 110% of the invoice value. Our insurance company is a state-operated enterprise enjoying high prestige in settling claims promptly and equitably and has agents in all main ports and regions of the world. Should any damage occur to the goods you might file your claim with their agent at your end, who will take up the matter without delay.

We insure the goods against the usual risks and in the present case All Risks. Should broader coverage be required, the extra premium is for the buyer's account.

We hope you will agree to our suggestion and look forward to your favourable reply.

Yours faithfully,
(signature)

Chapter 9 Insurance

Notes

1. state-operated 国营的
   state-owned 国营的
   private-operated 私营的
   private-owned 私营的
2. enjoying high prestige 享有很高的声望
3. settling claims 理赔
4. file claims 提出索赔
5. take up the matter 相当于 deal with，着手处理
6. without delay 毫不延误
7. for the buyer's account 由买方支付，由买方承担

Specimen Letter 3 The Insured Asking for Quotation from the Insurer

Dear Sirs,

　　We are a Shanghai-based import & export company and going to ship 20 containers of household electrical appliances to Rome next week. We want to insure the goods with you, who we know has a prestigious position in the insurance industry, if the rate is within our expectation.

　　Would you please quote us your most favorable premium rate of the said goods for the insured value of US$100000 against All Risks plus War Risk? The insurance is from our warehouse to the port of Rome.

　　We are awaiting your information.

Yours faithfully,
(signature)

Notes

1. Shanghai-based 总部设在上海的
2. prestigious a. 有声望的
3. premium rate 保险费率

Part VII. Exercises

I. Translate the following terms and expressions:

A. Into Chinese:

1. in answer to
2. a franchise shop
3. in regard to insurance
4. ship...in bulk

5. in the absence of
7. in other words
9. subject to
6. risk of shortage
8. risk of leakage
10. serve your purpose

B. Into English:

1. 一切险
3. 水渍险
5. 平安险
7. 额外保险
9. 保险费率
2. 免赔率（额）
4. 明确指示
6. 惯例
8. 特殊附加险
10. 淡水雨淋险

II. Choose the best answer to complete each of the following sentences:

1. We are now replying to your letter of March 15 ____ insurance. Which of the following is NOT right?
   A. in regard to   B. with regard to   C. regarding   D. as regard

2. Please let us know your premium ____ which you cover insurance against All Risks.
   A. with   B. at   C. for   D. against

3. The extra premium will be charged ____ your account.
   A. to   B. at   C. on   D. with

4. We will effect insurance against All Risks as requested, charging premium and freight ____ the consignees.
   A. to   B. for   C. on   D. with

5. According to the nature of the cargo, this cover ____ a 5% franchise.
   A. is subject to   B. is subjected to
   C. subject to   D. subjected to

6. Do you ____ against All Risks and TPND on this item? Which of the following is NOT right here?
   A. insure   B. cover   C. cover insurance   D. insure us

7. We have insured the goods ____ 10% above the invoice value.
   A. with   B. at   C. for   D. on

8. Please inform us ____ the details of the shipment as soon as you ship the goods.
   A. with   B. for   C. on   D. of

9. In reply ____ your fax of October 16, we would like to give you the following information.
   A. to   B. with   C. of   D. for

10. The goods are ready for shipment, but we can not load them _____ of your L/C.

    A. with the absence of   B. at the absence of

    C. in the absence of   D. to the absence of

III. Translate the following sentences into English:

1. 我们得知我方电脑运往纽约的一切险费率为1.5%。能否在别处以更合理的费率投保？

2. 此费率为本地所有的大保险商所普遍接受。

3. 兹告知此险别可以投保，但保费略高。

4. 如果你们想按发票金额的130%投保，我们可以办理，但要收取额外的保险费。

5. 由于战争风险增加，战争险的保费也提高了很多。

6. 请将我方货物按20000美元的保值投保水渍险。

7. 我方要求你方为此批货物投保罢工、暴动、民变险（Strikes, Riots & Civil Commotions）。

8. 我们的惯例是按发票金额的110%投保平安险和战争险。

9. 为更好的推销，我们将免费给你方寄送样品。

10. 保单是一种契约，是承保人和投保人之间协议的证明。

IV. Write an English letter based on the following information:

1. 买方来函询问保险情况，现写信答复：

（1）对于以CIF价格成交的交易，我方通常根据1981年1月1日的海洋运输公物保险条款向中国人民保险公司投保一切险。若买方要求依据协会货物保险条款办理，我方可以照办，但两者保费的差额由对方支付。

（2）若买方想要投保附加险，我方可以代办，额外保费由买方支付。我方将把保险商出具的保费收据寄给对方。

（3）保险金额通常为发票金额的110%。如果买方要求增加，可以照办，但额外保费也将由买方支付。

（4）盼对方寄来订单。

2. 买方寄来CFR价订单一份，现写信答复：

（1）我方大部分客户都是以CIF价下订单，因为这样可以节省时间，简化手续。建议对方也采用此做法。

（2）告知对方我方通常是按发票金额的110%向中国人民保险公司办理保险。中保是家国营企业，享有理赔迅速、处理公正的盛誉，并在世界各主要港口和地区都有代理。如果发生货损，对方可向当地中保的代理提出索赔。

（3）向对方说明这次交易一切险即可。如果对方要求投保更多险别，额外保费由对方承担。

Chapter 10

Complaint and Claim

Chapter 10 Complaint and Claim

Task 1 Making Complaints or Claims

Part I. Introduction

Complaints or claims made by one company against another are normal in international trade. On execution of a sales contract, both the seller and the buyer must abide by the terms and conditions of the contract and strictly perform their respective obligations. If one of the parties breaches the contract, the other may run into trouble, or suffer great losses. In this case, the affected party can either request the defaulter to make sure that such things will not happen again, which is known as "complaint", or request him to make up his losses according to the relevant provisions under the contract, which is called "claim". Letters written concerning the above are known as complaint or claim letters.

There are two kinds of complaint being frequently made by buyers.

1. The genuine complaint of wrong goods sending, poor quality, late delivery and excessive price or not as agreed.

2. The fault-finding complaint as an excuse used to escape from performance of their contracts either because they no longer want the goods or because they have found that they can get them cheaper elsewhere.

During the process of a contract execution in international trade, if one party breaks the contract, the other party who has suffered losses has the rights to complain or claim on the party who breaks the contract according to the relevant terms of the contract. For any disputes arising from the execution of the contract, we can use different ways to settle the disputes. Normally, amicable settlement or conciliation is the first choice because it saves time and cost while maintaining good business relations. If amicable settlement does not lead to a satisfactory result, the parties concerned may seek for arbitration in which the arbitration award shall be final and binding upon both parties.

Part II. Writing Skills

A complaint letter usually follows the under mentioned outlines:

1. Regret the need to complain.

2. Give a detailed presentation of facts to explain what is wrong.

3. Refer to the inconvenience caused.

4. Suggest how the matter should be put right.

Every complaint, no matter how trivial it seems, is important to the person who makes it. It therefore requires a prompt answer or acknowledgement. The answer should be factual, courteous and fair.

When making a claim, observe the following points:

1. Inform the receiver of details related to the goods to be claimed.

2. Make clear what your claim is.

3. Request the action: a replacement, repair, refund or compensation.

The purpose of writing a letter of complaint or claim is to get better service or reasonable compensation instead of accusing the others. Thus, a complaint or claim letter must be written in a restrained and tactful way.

Part III. Sample Letters

Sample 1   Complaint about Inferior Quality

20 March 2001
Smith & Co., Ltd
12 Allan Street
London, UK
Dear Sirs,

　　Our order No.325 of 6 March for floorboard materials has now been delivered.

　　We have examined the shipment carefully and, to our great disappointment, we find that they are not of the quality we ordered.

　　The materials do not match the samples you sent us. The quality of some of them is so poor that we feel that a mistake has been made in making up the order.

　　The goods do not match the requirements of our company. We have, therefore, no choice but to ask you to take the materials back and replace them with materials of the quality we ordered.

　　We are very keen to resolve this matter amicably and looking forward to your early reply.

　　　　　　　　　　　　　　　　　　　　　　　　　　　　Yours faithfully,

　　　　　　　　　　　　　　　　　　　　　　　　　　　　　　(signature)

Chapter 10 Complaint and Claim

Notes

1. to our great disappointment   令我们很失望的是

2. making up the order   备货，配制订单

3. replace   即 take the place of，取代，替代，代替，更换

4. be keen to do sth   热心于做某事，渴望做某事

Sample 2   Claim for Poor Packing

Dear Sirs,

　　We refer to sales contract No.258 covering the purchase of 180 metric tons of white cement.

　　We telexed you on 13 April informing you that the consignment arrived on 8 April.

　　On inspection, we found that 90 bags had burst and that the contents, estimated at 4500 kg, had been irretrievably lost.

　　We proceeded to have a survey report made. The report has now confirmed our initial findings.

　　The report indicates that the loss was due to the use of substandard bags for which you, the suppliers, are responsible.

　　On the strength of the survey report, we hereby register our claim against you as follows:

Short delivered quantity US$120

Survey charges US$30

Total claimed US$150

We enclose survey report No.278 and look forward to your early settlement of the claim.

　　　　　　　　　　　　　　　　　　　　　　　　Yours faithfully,

　　　　　　　　　　　　　　　　　　　　　　　　　　(signature)

Notes

1. on inspection   经检验

2. survey report   调查报告

3. substandard   标准以下的，不合标准的

4. on the strength of

(1) 一般意为"because of"，"因为，根据，凭借，基于某事物"，本文中即为此意。

　　e.g. I chose the shipping company and the insurance company on the strength of the importer's advice.

　　　我根据进口商的意见选择了船运和保险公司。

(2) 有时又意为"in the likelihood of"，"因……可能……"。

e.g. I searched some price information of local suppliers on the strength of the possible inquiries from international buyers.

因国际买家可能会来询盘，我先了解了一下本地供应商的价格信息。

5. register a claim against sb　向某人提出索赔

常用的表达为：

lodge (file/raise/make/ register) a claim against sb. for… (reason) for… (amount) on… (goods)

对……（货物）因……（原因）向某人提出……（金额）的索赔

accept a claim　接受索赔

entertain a claim　受理索赔

reject a claim　拒绝索赔

dismiss a claim　驳回索赔

settle a claim　理赔

withdraw a claim　撤回索赔

Sample 3　Claim for Short Delivery

Dear Sirs,

　　Order No.276 for 6000 Dozen Baseball Masks

We now inform you that the subject goods arrived here on May 26.

Unfortunately, upon opening the cartons, we found 48 dozen short-delivered. The cartons themselves remained intact, so we can only presume that the shortage must have occurred before shipment. Enclosed is a list of the quantities received, which please check with our order and the copy of your invoice.

As we had promised our customers the full quantity of 6000 dozen to catch the selling season, it will be highly appreciated if you will arrange for an immediate dispatch of the goods short-delivered to make up the quantity ordered.

We are looking forward to your early favorable reply.

Yours faithfully,

International Sportswear Manufacturing Co., Ltd.

Notes

1. short delivery　短交

Chapter 10 Complaint and Claim

short shipment   短装

short weight   短重

short-delivered   *adj.* 少交的，短交的

short-shipped   *adj.* 少装的，短装的

short-landed   *adj.* 少卸的，短卸的

2. baseball mask   棒球面罩

3. intact   *adj.* 完整的，未受损的

4. presume   *vt.* 认为，推测

5. make up   弥补；补齐，补足

   e.g. You're requested to make up the boxes short-delivered.
   请你方补齐短装的几箱货。

   make up an order   备齐订货

Sample 4 Claim on Damaged Goods

Dear Sirs,

On arrival of S.S. Victoria at our port yesterday, we took delivery of the 2000 cases of Coffee Sets covered by our Order No.183 immediately.

Much to our regret, it was found upon examination that the cases used were not strong enough to protect the goods with the result that the contents of forty cases were badly damaged and unfit for sale. Such being the case, we can't but ask you to send us replacements immediately and compensate us US$18950 for the loss sustained on the strength of the survey report issued by the Beijing Exit and Entry Inspection & Quarantine Bureau.

We have so far been satisfied with your execution of our orders and hope this incident is an exception. Please see to it that all our future orders are properly packed and can stand rough handling in transit.

We are holding the above goods at your disposal.

Yours faithfully,

(signature)

Notes

1. take delivery of   提货，收货，取货

2. upon examination   经检查

3. content   *n.* 内容，内部所有之物

4. such being the case 事实既然如此，情况既然如此

5. can't but 只得

6. sustain *vt.* 蒙受，遭受

7. on the strength of 凭借，根据

8. survey report 检验报告

9. the Beijing Exit and Entry Inspection & Quarantine Bureau
   北京出入境商品检验检疫局

10. rough handling 粗鲁搬运，野蛮操作

11. in transit 在运输途中

12. at one's disposal 由某人处理

Task 2　Reply to Complaints and Claims

Part I. Introduction

Letters in reply to the complaints or claims should always be courteous. Even if the complaint is unfounded, the sellers should not say so until they have good and reliable grounds to repudiate the complaint.

There are some rules for your reference:

1. The first thing to be decided is whether the complaint is justified. If it is so, the seller has to admit it readily, express his or her regret and agree to the buyer's request.

2. If the complaint or claim is not justified, point it out politely in an agreeable manner. It would be a wrong policy to reject the customer's request without any explanation.

3. If the seller cannot deal with a complaint promptly, acknowledge it at once and explain that the matter is being investigated and full reply will be sent later.

To sum up, firstly, put yourself in the customer's place—perhaps the customer realizes that his request is not a reasonable one. In that case, your refusal will not be annoying. Secondly, usually along with the refusal you can suggest an alternative that the customer will find reasonable. Thirdly, sometimes it is a matter of language—instead of writing in a negative tone, try to make it positive.

Part II. Writing Skills

When replying to complaints, plan your letter as follows:

1. Begin with a reference to the date of the original letter of complaint.

2. Apologize for the inconvenience caused.

Chapter 10 Complaint and Claim

3. Indicate what steps you are taking to set the matter right.

4. Express your expectations for further cooperation.

After receiving a claim from the buyer, the seller should deal with the matter without delay. Replies to claims usually contain the following points:

1. Confirm receipt of the claim.

2. Express your concern over what has happened.

3. Give the way to settle the problem: grant the claim or decline the claim.

4. If granting the claim, let the receiver know what actions have been taken and end your letter with assurance and desire for future development.

5. If declining the claim, explain the reasons and offer some friendly advice (to take the sting out of the denial), and conclude your letter with desire for future business.

Sample 1   Claim Accepted

Dear Mr. Johnson,

　　We have received your letter of Sep. 11th complaining about the raincoats supplied to your order No.1234.

　　Your letter has caused us a great deal of concern. We immediately tested a number of raincoats from the production batch you referred to and we regret to say that they are not perfect. The defects have been traced to a fault in one of the machines and this has now been put right.

　　We are arranging to send you 200 raincoats to replace the faulty 150 pieces. The extra 50 pieces we are sending you are free of charge. It is appreciated if you can return the faulty raincoats to us, carriage forward.

　　Please accept our sincere apologies for the inconvenience and trouble this matter has caused you. We hope that our above arrangement will meet with your approval and that you will continue placing orders with us as before.

　　Waiting for your confirmation.

Best Regards,
Wang Hao

Notes

1. production batch　生产批次

　　batch　一批，一组，一群；（食物、药物等的）一批生产的量；成批作业

2. trace to　找出……的所在，追踪到……，找到……的根源，追溯到

3. free of charge 免费

4. carriage forward 运费未付，运费由收件人支付，运费到付

5. as before 与以往一样，与以前一样

Sample 2 Claim Rejected

Dear Sirs,

　　We are in receipt of your letter of 5th June complaining about the glassware shipped to you by S.S. Victory.

　　We have looked into the matter in our records and could only find that the goods in question were in perfect condition when they left here. Therefore, the damage you complained about must have been caused by some fault on the part of the shipping company. Under such circumstance, we would advise you to file your claim with them for your loss.

　　However, if requested, we shall be glad to approach the shipping company on your behalf with a view to recovering damages from them as soon as possible.

　　　　　　　　　　　　　　　　　　　　　　　　Yours faithfully,

　　　　　　　　　　　　　　　　　　　　　　　　　　(signature)

Notes

1. look into 观察，调查

2. in question 正被考虑或讨论

3. in perfect condition 状况完好

   in good/bad condition 状况良好/不佳

4. on the part of 由某人做出，相当于 on sb's part

5. under such circumstance 在这种情况下

   类似表达：on such occasion, in this case

6. file a claim with/against sb for sth 就某事向某人提出索赔

7. on sb's behalf 等同于 on the behalf of sb，代表某人，为了某人

8. with a view to 为了……的目的

Sample 3 Settlement of Claim

Dear Sirs,

　　Your Claim on "Hero" Brand 100% Cotton Shirts

　　We have received your letter of 9th September, in which you put in a claim for a short

Chapter 10 Complaint and Claim

delivery of 50 dz. of "Hero" Brand 100% Cotton Shirts.

After checking with the manufacturers, we find that a mistake was made in packing though every possible attention has been paid to all your orders, for which please accept our sincere apologies.

50 dozen shirts have been sent to you by airmail today. Furthermore, we are sending you herewith as requested a check for US$1250 to compensate you for your loss. We believe our settlement of the claim will satisfy you to the full.

We assure you that we will take all necessary steps to prevent recurrence of similar things in future and hope to receive further orders from you.

Yours faithfully,
(signature)

Notes

1. to the full 完全地，充分地
2. take all necessary steps 采取所有必要的措施
3. prevent *vt.* 阻止，妨碍
   prevent sb. from doing sth. 阻止某人做某事
4. recurrence *n.* 再发生，复发
5. further orders 再次订货，进一步订购

Sample 4 Settlement of the Claim for Improper Packing and Short Weight

Dear Sirs,

Re: Your Contract No.315 for 1,200 M/T Chemical Fertilizer

We acknowledge receipt of your letter claiming on the consignment in question for improper packing and short weight.

We immediately got into this matter and studied your survey reports No.F138 and F139 together with your statement of claims. It was found that some 16 bags had not been packed in 5-ply strong paper bags as stipulated in the contract, thus resulting in the breakage during transit, for which we tender our apologies. We also found that our chemical fertilizer had been properly weighed at the time of loading.

So short weight is attributable to rough handling by the steamship company. You may claim against them for recovery of the loss.

> In view of our long-standing business relations, we will make payment by cheque for US$1850, the amount of one part of your claims, into your account with the Bank of China, upon receipt of your agreement.
>
> We trust that the arrangement we have made will satisfy you and look forward to receiving your further orders.
>
> Yours faithfully,
(signature)

Notes

1. acknowledge *v.* 告知收到（信件，礼物等）

2. get into   调查，仔细审查

3. some   *adv.* 大约

   e.g. We have sold some 40 tons of chemical fertilizer.
   　　我们约售出40吨化肥。

4. 5-ply   五层

   ply   *n.* 厚度，股

   three-ply wood   三夹板

   a two-ply rope   一根双股的绳子

5. is attributable to   可能归因于

   同 attributed to 比较，前者语气不确定，后者表明已有确凿的证据认为某事应归因于……。

6. rough handling   野蛮装卸

7. in transit   运输途中

8. in view of   鉴于

9. long-standing business relations   长期业务关系

Part IV. Useful Expressions and Typical Sentences

Useful Expressions

1. put in/lodge/file/register/make/lay/raise a claim against sb.   向某人索赔

2. claim... (a certain amount of money) from... (sb.) for ... (sth.)
   向……就……索赔……金额

3. make a claim against... (sb.) for... (a certain amount of money) for...
   向……就……（原因）索赔……金额

4. entertain/accept a claim   接受索赔

Chapter 10 Complaint and Claim

5. settle a claim   理赔，进行赔偿

6. survey report   检验报告

7. on the strength of...   因为/凭借……

8. on arrival of...   在……到达后

9. replacement goods   替换品

10. cannot but   只得

11. short delivery   短量；货少运了

12. short weight   短重；货不够秤

13. inferior quality   质量低劣

14. improper packing   不适当的包装

15. A is attributable to B   A 是由 B 引起/导致的

16. the time limit for claim   索赔期限

17. within... days after arrival of the goods   货物到达后……天内

18. go into the matter   调查此事

19. the survey charges   检验费

20. total amount of claim   索赔总额

Typical Sentences

1. The claim is to be lodged within 45 days after the arrival of the consignment at the destination port.

2. The claim must be accompanied by a survey report for seller's reference.

3. After looking into the matter, the surveyors find that the damage was caused by rough handling at the dock.

4. We are entitled to register a claim for at least 30% of the invoice value for inferior quality against the exporter.

5. Short weight is what the claim is for.

6. The goods you are claiming damaged were in perfect condition when they left the loading port, as can be evidenced by the B/L which is printed the word "Clean".

7. The discrepancy between the goods shipped and the original sample is unacceptable since the S/C stipulated the term of "sales by sample".

8. We have no choice but to file a claim on you, which we hope will receive your prompt attention.

9. After inspection the goods shipped are found not in conformity with the sample you sent to us.

10. We insist that you compensate the sum of our losses which were due to your improper packing.

11. Your claim is not acceptable because the date, July 31, 2007, when you raised it, has passed the time limit for a claim as stipulated in the contract No.123.

12. We hope you can understand that we would not have lodged the claim if we could afford to carry the loss.

13. If the claim is not resolved in the near future we will be compelled to resort to a lawsuit.

14. To settle your claim, we agree to make a reduction of 20% of the invoice value, which we think can make up your loss.

15. We will proceed to settle the claim by arbitration should you not accept our proposed solution, which is our maximum concession.

16. We regret that we have to cancel our order because of the inferior quality of your products. We ask you to cover any loss which might be caused as a result of the cancellation of the order.

17. We were very sorry to receive your complaint that the material you received was not of the quality expected.

18. The packing inside the case was too loose with the result that there was some shifting of the contents and several cups and plates have been broken. The attached list will give you details.

19. Your shipment of our order No.298 has been found short weight by 1000kg, for which we must file a claim amounting to US$800 plus inspection fee.

20. We are most anxious to compensate you for the shortage in weight mentioned in your letter of July 13 by offering you an allowance of 5%.

Part V. Project Training

Project 1

Training Situation:

China National Machinery Imp. & Exp. Corporation, Shanghai Branch signed a contract with an Italian importer in March, 2003 for the supply of 300 sets of Compressor. The contract stipulated that the Compressor should be packed in wooden cases lined with waterproof paper

Chapter 10 Complaint and Claim

and foam plastics. However, when the goods reached the importer on August 29, 2003, it was found upon examination that 30 sets were seriously damaged.

Training Requirements:

The students are required to write several letters according to the above situation:

1. A letter from the importer to the exporter lodging a claim against the latter.

2. A letter from the exporter to the importer accepting his claim for US$16000 for the damaged goods.

3. A letter from the exporter to the importer declining his claim for US$16000 for the damaged goods.

Project 2

Training Situation:

ABC Company received shipment of their Order No.123 from XYZ Company. But when deconsolidating the container, they found that cartons No.59-60 and 60-60 were missing. They checked the bill of lading, and it is marked "shipper's load and count". That means that the carrier was not responsible for the loss. As the value involved was not enough to entail survey or an arbitration or litigation action, they wanted to settle the problem amicably with the seller, XYZ Company.

Training Requirements:

Suppose that you work for ABC Company. Write a claim letter based on the above situation.

Part VI. Optional Study

I. Related Information

Accuracy is important in business. However, mistakes do happen. Customers may sometimes receive damaged or defective merchandise, be overcharged at wrong prices, receive their ordered goods too late, or not at all. There are lots of reasons that cause customers to complain.

Claim as a noun is defined as a demand for something that somebody has a right to or owns. Claim as a verb is defined as to demand attention or to force somebody to give attention. A claim letter, therefore, is a demand from a customer for something that is due or owed, or something that is a correction of a problem.

A claim should be made as quickly as possible for it can be rejected if it is too late. Some companies have a deadline for claims. For example, you may sometimes read "you must make any claim within two weeks of arrival of goods", or, "claims must be made immediately upon delivery".

To get a proper response, a claim letter must be brief and clear. The issues of complaint must be specified or listed, and acceptable solutions to the problem or requested actions must be spelled out or listed unless you are willing to let the company decide what actions they will take.

Generally, a customer may complain about:

1. an incorrect bill, invoice, or statement

2. a bill for merchandise ordered but never received

3. delivery of unordered merchandise

4. delivery of incorrect merchandise

5. delivery of damaged or defective merchandise

6. an unusually delayed delivery

Complaint or claims could be settled through amicable discussion by both parties. In case no settlement can be reached between two parties, the case under disputes can be submitted for arbitration to be held in the country where the defendant resides. The arbitral award is accepted as final and binding upon both parties. The arbitration fees shall be borne by the losing party.

II. Supplementary Specimen Letters

Specimen Letter 1

Dear Sirs,

The shipment of our order No.235 for the whole set of equipment for recording used for a professional recording studio has been duly received. Thanks for your prompt delivery.

Everything seemed perfect and amicable before the case No.16 was unpacked. This case contained a sound mixer, the essential part of the whole system. Much to our regret, due to the negligent packing, the mixer was damaged to such an extent that it is totally unusable. We hereby enclose the photos of its present appearance together with a survey report of a qualified surveyor. Regarding the importance of the sound mixer in making the whole system workable, we must request your immediate replacement of it.

Awaiting your favorable reply as soon as possible at your earliest convenience.

Yours faithfully,

(signature)

Chapter 10 Complaint and Claim

Notes

1. the whole set of equipment for recording used for a professional recording studio   职业摄录专用的成套录音设备

2. sound mixer   混音器

3. negligent packing   包装方面的疏忽

Specimen Letter 2

Dear Sirs,

Subject: CONTRACT NO.23HBSF/1008CN

The T-shirt under the above contract which you shipped on May 22, 2008 were delivered by the vessel today. After inspected by the Port Office of SGS, we found some of the cartons are broken and some of the T-shirts are dirty.

This is the second time in two weeks we write to you about the same matter and we find it hard to understand why precautions could not be taken to prevent a repetition of the earlier damage.

Although not all the goods are in bad conditions, this second experience within such a short time suggests that the cartons' quality is not so good or the cartons are carried roughly. We hope that in handling our future orders you will bear this in mind.

The T-shirts are usable, but because of their condition we can't sell them at the normal price and suggest you make us an allowance of 10% at the invoice cost. If you can't do this, then I am afraid we shall have to return the T-shirts for replacement.

Waiting for your early reply.

Yours faithfully,

Park Junshou

Encl: Inspection of Quality

Notes

1. bear ... in mind   把……牢记在心
2. SGS，是 Societe Generale de Surveillance 的简称，译为"通用鉴定公司或通用公证行"。它创建于 1887 年，是目前世界上最大、资格最老的民间第三方从事产品质量控制和技术鉴定的跨国公司。总部设在日内瓦，在世界各地设有 251 家分支机构，256 个专业实验室和 27000 名专业技术人员，在 142 个国家开展产品质检、监

控和保证活动。据该公司宣称，目前世界上有 23 个国家（主要是发展中国家）的政府实施 SGS 检验，包括：安哥拉、阿根廷、玻利维亚、布基那法索、布隆迪、柬埔寨、喀麦隆、中非、刚果共和国、象牙海岸、厄瓜多尔、几内亚、肯尼亚、马拉维、马里、毛里塔尼亚、墨西哥、巴拉圭、秘鲁、菲律宾、卢旺达、塞内加尔、刚果民主共和国、赞比亚。他们基于对 SGS 的公正性、科学性、权威性和技术能力的充分信任，委托 SGS 对进口货物实施"装船前全面监管计划"（Comprehensive Import Super-vision Scheme，简称 CISS），可抑制非法的进出口活动。

Specimen Letter 3

Dear Sirs,

　　The shipment of men's shirts arrived yesterday and it was noticed that part of the cartons were wet. We immediately had all the consignments examined by a local qualified surveyor with the presence of the shipping company's representative.

　　On the strength of the survey report it was evidenced that 6 out of 10 cartons were totally wet from sea water. Each carton was invoiced containing 10 dozen plastic bags with each wrapping a shirt. Therefore 60 dozen shirts have been soaked by sea water and have lost a great deal of quality. Such loss is due to the bad weather in transit, which we have insured against, and should be compensated for by the insurer.

　　Since the insurance policy is in your hand now, would you please file a claim against the insurer at once? Enclosed with this letter please find the survey report and the statement of the shipping company's representative, which will be essential proof for the claim.

　　We hope the process of the claim will be smooth. Thanks in advance for your handling of this situation on our behalf.

　　　　　　　　　　　　　　　　　　　　　　　　　　Yours faithfully,

　　　　　　　　　　　　　　　　　　　　　　　　　　　　(signature)

Notes

1. "it was noticed that ..." 相当于 "we noticed that ..."。之所以用被动语态有两点考虑，其一是突出客观性，其二是不一味地使用主动语态以增加表达的多样性。常用的例子有：it is/was found out that ... ; it is/was heard that ... ; it is/was revealed that ... 以及 it is known that ... 等。

2. "with the presence of" 意为"当着……的面"或"在……在场的情况下"。

3. it was evidenced that　据证实，证明，显示，表明

Chapter 10 Complaint and Claim

4. Each carton was invoiced … 此句译作"发票显示……。"国际贸易中的商业发票比起只写商品名及单价、总价的国内零售发票要复杂些，一般来说还要写上货物的包装情况、运输标志、信用证或销售合同号码及货物装卸港等信息。

Part VII. Exercises

I. Translate the following terms and expressions:

A. Into Chinese:

1. settlement of your claim
2. upon their arrival
3. survey report
4. surveyor
5. in perfect condition
6. Entry-Exit Inspection and Quarantine Bureau
7. at one's disposal
8. defective
9. unexpected events
10. convey their apologies

B. Into English:

1. 向某人索赔
2. 复验
3. 无法销售的
4. 未执行订单
5. 给某人造成很大麻烦
6. 实行严格控制
7. 合同价格降3%
8. 鉴于
9. 为某原因索赔
10. 接受索赔

II. Choose the best answer to complete each of the following sentences:

1. The packing is insufficient and the ____ leak out considerably.
   A. inside   B. material   C. goods   D. contents

2. A close inspection and a careful test by Shanghai Entry-Exit Inspection and Quarantine Bureau showed that some amplifiers (扩音器) are ____ damaged.
   A. badly   B. bad   C. perfect   D. well

3. Much to our astonishment, nearly 30% of the electronic components ____ water stained.
   A. find   B. found   C. were found   D. have found

4. The damage to the machine tools occurred ____ transit, so you should lodge a claim against the insurance company.
   A. at   B. in   C. for   D. with

5. Considering our good relations, we are prepared to allow you 5% ____ the original price.
   A. off   B. reduction   C. low   D. lower than

6. We have a clean bill of lading to prove that the goods were received by the carrier in _____ condition. Therefore, they must have been damaged en route.

    A. badly   B. terrible   C. well   D. perfect

7. It would be unfair if the loss be totally imposed on as the liability rests ___both parties. But we are ready to meet you half way, i.e., 50% of the loss only.

    A. with   B. against   C. for   D. of

8. You can approach ___the insurance company ___the shipping company for claim, as the liability rests with them.

    A. neither, nor   B. both, and   C. either, or   D. either, nor

9. We are heavily ___at the moment, and we regret we cannot advance shipment of your order.

    A. committed   B. crushed   C. burdened   D. promised

10. Our goods have been weighed carefully before shipping and we have _____ that full weight was delivered.

    A. certificate   B. document   C. evidence   D. inspection

III. Fill in the blanks with proper prepositions:

1. The buyers are complaining _____ the wrong goods _____the sellers.

2. We are holding the goods of faulty goods _____ your disposal.

3. As the damage occurred during transit, please direct your claim _____ the insurance company.

4. Our clients have claimed _____us _____ delayed delivery of the goods.

5. We regret to say that we have to lodge our claim _____ the Arbitration Committee.

6. This delay is causing us serious inconvenience because we promise delivery _____ the strength of your assurance.

7. The shipment is short-invoiced _____ ￥8600 and we have drawn a draft on you _____ the balance.

8. Please cable your confirmation on receipt of our remittance for US$5,000 in settlement _____the claim.

IV. Complete the following sentences in English:

1. _____ (货物短缺) is due to confusion in packing.

2. You should _____(对……负责任) the loss of the goods in transit.

Chapter 10 Complaint and Claim

3. I'd like to talk with you about 2 tons _____(白糖短重).

4. _____(鉴于我们长期的业务关系) we'll give you this accommodation.

5. We are regretful that we have to _____(向你方提出索赔).

6. We are sending you a Survey Report_____(由上海商品检验局签发的) under separate cover.

V. Translate the following sentences into English:

1. 我们已邀请保险公司检验箱子和箱内所装的货，该检验员认为损坏事故系包装不牢所致。

2. 在 CIF 条件下，我方不承担货物运上船前的一切风险。

3. 我们同意通过降低我们新合同的价格来弥补你们的损失。

4. 我方已与承保人联系了，但他们拒绝承担任何责任。他们把损失归咎于长时间海运途中的潮湿天气。

5. 你方货物抵达我方时，严重受损，根本无法销售。

6. 我认为损失不是在运输途中，就是在装运前发生的。

7. 由于你方提供的证据不充分，因此我们不接受你方索赔。

8. 由于责任不在我方，因此我们拒绝索赔。

9. 货物抵达后，我们进行了仔细检查，发现部分袋子质量不佳。

10. 我们第 369 号订单的货物经查短重 300 公斤，现在向你们索赔 800 美元，包括检验费在内。

VI. Fill in the blanks with proper words, with the initial letters given:

Dear Sirs,
    We have duly received your letter of September 13 and much regret to n_____ that the above goods suffered serious d ____ in consequences of a fire to the carrying vessel on r _____. The c _____ is insured with the People's Insurance Company of China. J_____ by the circumstances leading to the fire, the loss f _____ under the insurance cover and should be indemnified by the I ____. We f_____ sure that you have l____ your claim with the a ____ for the insurer.
    In the event that, as a r ____ of the damage to the shipment in q ____, another lot is required as replenishment , kindly telex the q ____ desired, when we shall submit our offer for your c_____.
    We look forward to your early reply.

                                                                Yours faithfully,
                                                                (signature)

VII. Translate the following letter into English:

负责人：

  我们十分遗憾地得知有 10 台洗衣机因木箱损坏而受损。可这并非我们的过错。首先，我们用以装运洗衣机的木箱是为出口特制的，你们可以看到箱子上有指定的检验员签发的"出口包装"的标签。其次，这批货物上的清洁提单完全证明装运时状况完好。因此，显而易见，木箱的损坏是由于运输途中或在你们港口卸货时的粗暴搬运。在此情况下，我们不能为此负责。由于此货投保了一切险，我们建议你方尽快向保险公司索赔。当然，我们会尽我们所能来协助你们取得赔偿。

谨上

VIII. Write an English letter based on the following information:

The shipment of the glassware you ordered has arrived, but a number of the wooden cases and contents inside were found broken. The survey report from the Entry-Exit Inspection and Quarantine Bureau shows that the breakage is due to bad stowage (装货方法)—the cases containing the glassware are put under machines in the same hold (船舱). You claim for $8000. But you need to decide first against whom you should file the claim.

Chapter 11

Fax & E-mail

Part I. Introduction

1. Introduction to Fax

Fax, which is short for facsimile machine, is a very modern communication service. The fax machine which is now installed in most companies, corporations and unite, even in some families is quite easy to be operated. The fax machine is a device that can send or receive pictures and text over a telephone line. Fax machines work by digitizing an image—dividing it into a grid of dots. Each dot is either on or off, depending on whether it is black or white.

The first fax machine was invented by Scottish mechanic and inventor Alexander Bain. However, Fax machines did not become popular with consumers until the 1980s.

Many inventors after Alexander Bain worked hard on inventing and improving fax machine type devices.

The use of fax machines has greatly impacted the history of the world over the last 160 years.

Some of the features that differentiate one fax machine from another include the following:

Speed: Fax machines transmit data at different rates, from 4800 bps to 28800 bps. A 9600-bps fax machine typically requires 10 to 20 seconds to transmit one page.

Printer type: Most fax machines use a thermal printer that requires special paper that tends to turn yellow or brown after a period. More expensive Fax machines have printers that can print on regular bond paper.

Paper size: The thermal paper used in most fax machines comes in two basic sizes: 8.5-inches wide and 10.1-inches wide. Some machines accept only the narrow-sized paper.

Paper cutter: Most fax machines include a paper cutter because the thermal paper that most fax machines use comes in rolls. The least expensive models and portable faxes, however, may not include a paper cutter.

Paper feed: Most fax machines have paper feeds so that you can send multiple-page documents without manually feeding each page into the machine.

Autodialing: Fax machines come with a variety of dialing features. Some enable you to program the fax to send a document at a future time so that you can take advantage of the lowest telephone rates.

2. Introduction to E-mail

In computer terms, E-mail is short for electronic mail. This phenomenon did not become popular until 1990 and now it is a main business and personal communications. E-mail is cheaper and faster than a letter, less intrusive than a phone call, less hassle than a fax. Using E-mail, differences in location and time zone are less of an obstacle to communication. There is also evidence that E-mail leads to a more egalitarian information structure. Because of these advantages, E-mail using is exploding in business field.

E-mail began as an experiment by the military to be able to send and from the battlefield. Thus was born E-mail or electronic-mail.

The first E-mail was sent in 1972 using two machines by an engineer named Ray Tomlinson. Later he wrote a mail program for Tenex, the BBN-grown operating system that, by now, was running on most of the ARPANET's PDP-10 machines. The mail program was written in two parts: (1)to send messages, you would use a program called SNDMSG; (2)to receive mail, you would use the other part called READMAIL.

A difference between E-mail and other medias is that what the sender sees when composing a message might not look like what the reader sees. Your message's visual qualities may be quite different by the time it gets to someone else's screen.

E-mail has had a wonderful impact on the amount of information being sent world wide. It is now an important method of transmitting information previously sent by regular mail, telephone, courier, fax, television, or radio.

E-mail can also be abused by companies who think that they can use the Internet as an advertisement opportunity. Many companies send unsolicited mail known as spam. The U.S. Congress passed a law in 2003 that was designed to curb spam. This law makes it illegal to send messages that use deceptive subject lines and false return addresses, proving fines for as much as $6 million and possible prison terms for violators:

E-mail is used extensively for personal communication, from within an office as well as from one person to another, from office to office within the same country, and overseas. The most used E-mail programs are Outlook Express and Microsoft Office Outlook. The general principles for sending E-mail are the same:

1. Enter your E-mail package.

2. Click on the New Mail button which will display the New Message window.

3. Click in the "To" box and type the name of the person you are sending the E-mail to. Ensure that you have keyed in the address exactly.

4. Click on the Send button to send the E-mail message.

The importance of good writing skills:

1. Customers see your writing more than they see you.

2. Good writing skills show that you really care.

3. Good writing skills contribute more forcefully to arguments/persuasion/selling.

4. Good writing skills reduce risk of losing a customer or damaging a customer relationship, and foster good relationships with colleagues.

Part II. Structures and Samples

1. Structure of Fax

The layout of fax is simple and the message is same as a letter. It has the following points:

(1) It can be communicated as fast as international phone call.

(2) It is much cheaper than an international phone call.

(3) Pictures, charts, etc., can be sent by the machine easily as well.

(4) It is a 24-hour service and the message can be received unattended.

A fax form is used to send information to another department, branch or company through a facsimile machine. A "cover" sheet is the first sheet of the fax and contains the following information:

- whom the fax is to (name of person and company)
- whom the fax is from
- the fax number you are sending the fax to
- the date of the fax
- your fax number (this is often printed at the top of the sheet)
- the number of pages, including the cover, so the receiver knows how many pages have been sent

Chapter 11 Fax & E-mail

Sample 1

Facsimile

To(致): Robert Yates & Co., Ltd

Attn(送呈): Office Manager

FROM: Julia Donaldson

DATE: 12 May, 2000

Fax(传真号码): 3789056

SUBJECT: Installation of Software

NO. OF PAGES (incl. cover): 1

I wish to confirm that I will be at your office at 9 a.m. tomorrow to install your Office 2000 program.

Sample 2

FACSIMILE TRANSMISSION

To: Johnson Company

Attn.: Eric Lee

From: Simon Davis

Date: May 23, 1993

Fax: 2215706

Your Ref: 2051/ef

Our Ref: 5237/nl

Subject:

CC: Kate Long

Pages: 1

Dear Sirs,

    We are an American company, our shares are to be issued next month. Our company is to be granted a World Bank credit soon. Should you be interested in cooperation or in buying our shares, please do not hesitate to contact us.

> We look forward to hearing from you.
>
> Yours Sincerely,
>
> Simon Davis
>
> Managing Director

2. Structure of E-mail

E-mails consist of the following parts:

1. the sender's E-mail address

2. the receiver's E-mail address

3. the subject

4. the CC's-mail address (optional)

5. the Blind Carbon Copy's address (optional)

6. body

7. attachment (optional)

How to write an E-mail:

1. Focus immediately on the information you need. Make your main idea at or near the opening of the E-mail.

2. Tell why you need the information if the reason is not obvious.

3. Emphasize due dates. Phrases such as: "at your earliest convenience" or "as soon as possible" seem polite, but they make it easy for the reader to delay answering. If you have a due date in mind, say so. Sometimes put the due date in a paragraph by itself for special emphasis.

4. Supply any further information, contact names and numbers, or forms so the reader can respond quickly and easily.

Sample 1

发件人：	zhanghua1967@gmail.com
收件人：	goodfurniture @hotmail.com
抄送：	Huangkun8@sina.com; gaowei@gmail.com
日期：	2010-2-19　17:37:21
主题：	Making business relationship

Dear Mr. Zhang,

We learn from the Commercial Counselor's office of the Embassy of the People's Republic of

China in Australia that your firm specializes in manufacturing furniture.

We now avail ourselves of this opportunity to write to you and see if we can establish business relations by a start of some practical transactions.

We look forward to getting your reply soon.

Sincerely,

Zhang Hua

Director

String Furniture Manufacturing Company

136 Evergreen Road, Huai'an   223003

Jiangsu, China

Tel:86-517-2336527

Fax:86-517-2336807

Sample 2

From：	shriamsteels@gmail.com
To：	Huangkun1967@hotmail.com
CC：	Huangkun8@sina.com,wangkun@longwill.biz
Date：	2008-2-19 17:37:21
Subjects：	No subject

Dear Susan,

We have received book returns from Hornsby College of 20 copies of No.214 Word Processing operators. They require No.222 Word Processing functions. Could you please arrange for books to be couriered to John Masters at Hornsby College, 24 View Road, Hornsby 22077.

Best Regards.

Tina

Cheryl price director

Soft publications PTY LTD

Part III. Useful Expressions and Typical Sentences

1. From and To 发送者和接收者

   A: What do you put on the fax cover page other than From and To?

   B: The title, total pages including the cover page, and telephone and fax numbers of each party.

   A：传真首页上除了发送者和接收者还写些什么？

   B：标题、页数、包括扉页、双方的电话号和传真号。

2. Fax it to me 传真给我

   A: Mike, the contract is signed by our GM. Do you want me to send it overnight?

   B: Yes, please. Could you also fax it to me now?

   A：迈克，我们总经理在合同上签字了，我要用特快专递发给你吗？

   B：是的，请发给我。你能不能现在就传真一份给我？

3. Fax template 传真格式

   A: Do we have a fax template of the company?

   B: We do. Ask Lisa to get an electronic copy.

   A：我们公司有统一的传真格式吗？

   B：有，去找丽莎要一个电子文档。

4. Followed by originals (contract) 续发原件（合同）

   A: Linda, I will fax the letter to you, followed by express mail of the originals.

   B: Thank you so much.

   A：琳达，我会传真一封信给你，再把原件用快递续发给你。

   B：非常感谢你。

5. Legally acceptable 法律承认的

   A: Can we use the faxed contract?

   B: It may not be legally acceptable. You can use it temporarily, but you need to get the originals ASAP.

   A: Why?

   B: Because faxed copy can have forged signatures.

   A：我们能使用传真的合同吗？

   B：法律上是无效的，你可以临时使用，但你应该尽快拿到原件。

   A：为什么？

   B：因为传真件上的签名可以伪造。

   注：ASAP is short for as soon as possible.

Chapter 11 Fax & E-mail

Part IV. Optional Study

How to Use E-mail Properly

In your E-mail or written communication, please avoid using the word "Don't" or "Can't". That may be regarded as rude and only use it when you want to show your anger or instruct an order. A better way instead is to use "Do not" or "Cannot". Besides, tips for E-mail communication includes content no more than 5-8 rows normally. Avoid writing an essay. Use point form whenever possible. Always state the word "Please" and "Thank you" as FIN or EMS is service provider. In some cases, you may use the "Subject" row above to draw people's attention. Write something key/important in the Subject box. Even you reply people's E-mail, do not simply press the Reply or Reply to all button, chop away those useless "gun fire exchange" E-mails attached and watch the reply distribution list whether they are fit to receive the E-mail or not. And also please revise the Subject box description if nature of the E-mail content is changed. Use zip function so that larger file are faster to transmit. Lastly, always use the Flag function setting deadline if you expect replies.

Part V. Exercises

I. Choose a sentence from A, B, C and D to fill the blanks:

1. Dear Macey,

Thanks for your monthly report, which I received a few days ago. I have read it carefully, but I am not clear about it. I hope you can explain.

__A__ the sales figures for Q2 are so much lower than the target figures? You do not really make this clear. Also, __B__ in more detail why not you have included the costs for the XYZ project in Q2.

Also, __C__ save the document as a reference file and email it to me again. One more thing, __D__ have it translated into Chinese by the end of week? That would be great. Thanks.

  A. Can you tell me why

  Do you think you could possibly tell me why

  Could you explain why

  Do you think you could let me know why

  B. I wonder if you could explain

  I was wondering if you could let me know

  C. I wonder if you could

  I was wondering if you could

D. Can you

   Do you think you could possibly

   Do you think you could

   Would it be possible for you to

   Could you

2. Dear Carol,

Thanks for your E-mail regarding your request for professional English training. Generally speaking, I think it is good idea and one that would help to improve the company workflow.

However, __A__ supply me with more information so that I can make a proper decision about it? __B__ you think you need the training and what the topic and content of the training will be? __C__ how long the training is going to last and where the training will be held? __D__ how much we are expected to pay for it and something about the company who is providing the training.

I look forward to hearing from you.

A. Can you

   Do you think you could possibly

   Do you think you could

   Would it be possible for you to

   Could you

B. Can you tell me why

   Do you think you could possibly tell me why

   Would it be possible for you to let me know why

   Could you explain why

   Do you think you could let me know why

C. Can you tell me

   Do you think you could possibly tell me

   I wonder it be possible for you to let me know

   Do you think you could let me know

D. I wonder if you could explain

   I was wondering if you could let me know

II. Read the clues and its translation, and then try to write an E-mail according to the clues:

This is writing to Julie to thank him for the proposal she has finished. Tim thinks the proposal is good, but he wants certain questions answered before he forwards the proposal to regional office for their approval:

1. What are Julie's growth estimates for next year?
2. What are the stages of the project and how are these stages to be implemented?
3. Who should lead to the project?

Tim wants to make a good impression on regional office, so he would like 15 professionally copies of the proposal in nice covers. He also wants translations of the proposal in Chinese, Japanese and Spanish.

III. Rearrange the order of sentences in the following letter:

Dear Emily,

(a)Please could you let me know what the engineer says, and how much the repair is going to cost by the end of this week? (b)If necessary, could you also change the paper. (c)The photocopier has broken down again. (d)I was wondering if you could call the supplier and ask then to come and check the machine and the paper. (e)We have recently changed our photocopying paper to a much cheaper brand, so I think it might have something to do with the new paper.

Thanks for your help.

Anita

IV. Read the following information and write an E-mail:

You work for a soap manufacturing company. Tests show that one of your new products is very bad for skin. Your boss wants to stop manufacturing the product and recall all the orders.

Write an E-mail to your overseas customer explaining the situation and asking them to return the units they bought last month. Ask them also for the contact details of any of their customers.

V. Fill in the table according to the following letter:

Letter A

Jan. 15, 2009

Dear Smith,

Your letter of credit No.345 covering your order No.123 for 40 metric tons of Ore has reached us this morning. Thank you.

After reading it thoroughly, we found that there is no stipulation of partial shipments being allowed in the L/C, so we can hardly manage to arrange this parcel. When making our offer No.234 dated December 5, we say clearly that the parcel is to be divided into 2 lots. That is: 20 metric tons for each.

    At present, the first lot of the goods is ready for shipment, so we have to request you to amend the L/C accordingly as soon as possible.

Yours faithfully,
Wang Dali
General Manager

Letter B

February 2, 2010

Dear Frank,

    Thanks for your E-mail. At this point, I will be available 2 p.m. on Monday. I hope this is OK for you.

Yours,
Tony

Letter A

FACSIMILE	
To:	
Attn:	
Fax:	
From:	
Date:	
NO. OF PAGES:	
Message:	

Chapter 11 Fax & E-mail

Letter B

	FACSIMILE
To:	
Attn:	
Fax:	
From:	
Date:	
NO. OF PAGES:	
Message:	

附录　外贸函电常用词汇

国际贸易

出口信贷　export credit
出口津贴　export subsidy
商品倾销　dumping
外汇倾销　exchange dumping
优惠关税　special preference
保税仓库　bonded warehouse
贸易顺差　favorable balance of trade
贸易逆差　unfavorable balance of trade
进口配额制　import quota
自由贸易区　free trade zone
对外贸易值　value of foreign trade
国际贸易值　value of international trade
普遍优惠制　generalized system of preferences (GSP)
最惠国待遇　most-favored nation treatment (MFNT)

价格条件

价格术语　trade term (price term)
运费　freight
单价　price
码头费　wharfage
总值　total value
卸货费　landing charges
金额　amount
关税　customs duty
净价　net price
印花税　stamp duty
含佣价　price including commission
港口税　port dues

回佣   rebate

装运港   port of shipment

折扣   discount /allowance

卸货港   port of discharge

批发价   wholesale price

目的港   port of destination

零售价   retail price

进口许口证   import licence

现货价格   spot price

出口许口证   export licence

期货价格   forward price

现行价格（时价）   current price prevailing price

国际市场价格   world (international) market price

离岸价（船上交货价）   FOB-free on board

成本加运费价（离岸加运费价）   C&F-cost and freight

到岸价（成本加运费、保险费价）   CIF-cost, insurance and freight

交货条件

交货   delivery

轮船   steamship(S.S)

装运/装船   shipment

租船   charter (the chartered ship)

交货时间   time of delivery

定程租船   voyage charter

装运期限   time of shipment

定期租船   time charter

托运人（一般指出口商）   shipper /consignor

收货人   consignee

班轮   regular shipping liner

驳船   lighter

舱位   shipping space

油轮   tanker

报关   clearance of goods

陆运收据　cargo receipt
提货　to take delivery of goods
空运提单　airway bill
正本提单　original BL
选择港（任意港）　optional port
选港费　optional charges
选港费由买方负担　optional charges to be borne by the Buyers 或 optional charges for Buyers' account
一月份装船　shipment during January /January shipment
一月底装船　shipment not later than Jan. 31st. /shipment on or before Jan. 31st.
一/二月份装船　shipment during Jan./Feb. 或 Jan./Feb. shipment
在……（时间）分两批装船　shipment during...in two lots
在……（时间）平均分两批装船　shipment during...in two equal lots
分三个月装运　in three monthly shipments
分三个月，每月平均装运　in three equal monthly shipments
立即装运　immediate shipments
即期装运　prompt shipments
收到信用证后 30 天内装运　shipments within 30 days after receipt of L/C
不允许/允许分批装船　partial shipment not allowed /partial shipment not permitted /partial shipment not unacceptable

交易磋商、合同签订

订单　indent
订货/订购　book /booking
电复　cable reply
实盘　firm offer
递盘　bid /bidding
递实盘　bid firm
还盘　counter offer
发盘（发价）　offer
发实盘　offer firm
询盘（询价）　inquiry /enquiry
指示性价格　price indication

速复　reply immediately
参考价　reference price
习惯做法　usual practice
交易磋商　business negotiation
不受约束　without engagement
业务洽谈　business discussion
限××复　subject to reply ××
限××复到　subject to reply reaching here ××
有效期限　time of validity
有效至××　valid till ××
购货合同　purchase contract
销售合同　sales contract
购货确认书　purchase confirmation
销售确认书　sales confirmation
一般交易条件　general terms and conditions
以未售出为准　subject to prior sale
需经卖方确认　subject to seller's confirmation
需经我方最后确认　subject to our final confirmation

贸易方式

INT /auction　拍卖
寄售　consignment
招标　invitation of tender
投标　submission of tender
一般代理人　agent
总代理人　general agent
代理协议　agency agreement
累计佣金　accumulative commission
补偿贸易　compensation trade
又叫：往返贸易　counter trade
　　　或抵偿贸易　compensating/compensatory trade
来料加工　processing on giving materials
来料装配　assembling on provided parts

独家经营/专营权　exclusive right

独家经营/包销/代理协议　exclusivity agreement

独家代理　sole agency/ sole agent/ exclusive agency/ exclusive agent

品质条件

品质	quality	原样	original sample
规格	specifications	复样	duplicate sample
说明	description	对等样品	counter sample
标准	standard type	参考样品	reference sample
商品目录	catalogue	封样	sealed sample
宣传小册	pamphlet	公差	tolerance
货号	article No.	花色（搭配）	assortment
样品	sample	增减	plus or minus

代表性样品　representative sample

大路货（良好平均品质）　fair average quality

商检仲裁

索赔	claim	争议	disputes
罚金条款	penalty	仲裁	arbitration
不可抗力	Force Majeure	仲裁庭	arbitral tribunal

产地证明书　certificate of origin

品质检验证书　inspection certificate of quality

重量检验证书　inspection certificate of weight (quantity)

商品检验局　commodity inspection bureau (C.I.B.)

品质、重量检验证书　inspection certificate

数量条件

个数	number	净重	net weight
容积	capacity	毛作净	gross for net
体积	volume	皮重	tare
毛重	gross weight	溢短装条款	more or less clause

外汇

外汇	foreign exchange	法定贬值	devaluation
外币	foreign currency	法定升值	revaluation

汇率　rate of exchange　　　　　　浮动汇率　floating rate
国际收支　balance of payments　　　硬通货　hard currency
直接标价　direct quotation　　　　　软通货　soft currency
间接标价　indirect quotation　　　　金平价　gold standard
买入汇率　buying rate　　　　　　　通货膨胀　inflation
卖出汇率　selling rate　　　　　　　固定汇率　fixed rate
金本位制度　gold standard　　　　　黄金输送点　gold points
铸币平价　mint par　　　　　　　　纸币制度　paper money system
国际货币基金　international monetary fund
黄金外汇储备　gold and foreign exchange reserve
汇率波动的官定上下限　official upper and lower limits of fluctuation

参 考 文 献

[1] 程同春. 新编国际商务英语函电[M]. 南京：东南大学出版社，2001.
[2] 刘惠玲，王俊. 国际商务函电[M]. 北京：对外经济贸易大学出版社，2002.
[3] 李宏亮. 国际商务函电[M]. 北京：对外经济贸易大学出版社，2008.
[4] 尹小莹. 外贸英语函电[M]. 西安：西安交通大学出版社，2004.
[5] 樊红霞，汪奠才. 英文外贸函电[M]. 北京：外语教学与研究出版社，2007.
[6] 苏根林. 实用商务英语函电[M]. 南京：东南大学出版社，2006.
[7] 梁平编. 外贸英文函电简明教程[M]. 广州：华南理工大学出版社，2002.
[8] 国际商务英语函电[M]. 北京：对外经济贸易大学出版社，2005.
[9] 徐美荣. 外贸英语函电[M]. 北京：对外经济贸易大学出版社，2007.
[10] 凌华倍，朱佩芬. 外经贸英语函电与谈判[M]. 北京：中国对外经济贸易出版社，2002.
[11] 邹建华，江峰. 实用进出口英语函电[M]. 北京：电子工业出版社，2005.
[12] 戚云方. 新编外贸英语函电与谈判[M]. 杭州：浙江大学出版社，2002.
[13] 戚云方. 外经贸英语写作与套语[M]. 杭州：浙江大学出版社，2002.
[14] 贺雪娟. 外贸函电实用英语[M]. 北京：高等教育出版社，2007.
[15] 黄霜林，梁媛媛. 国际商务函电实用教程[M]. 武汉：武汉理工大学出版社，2008.
[16] 张成伟. 外贸英语函电[M]. 北京：科学出版社，2008.
[17] 杨润辉，尹小莹. 外贸英语函电——商务英语应用文写作[M]. 西安：西安交通大学出版社，2008.
[18] 王元歌，刘辉. 商务英语阅读教程[M]. 北京：北京大学出版社，2007.